Community Spirit

A practical guide to collaborative language learning

**Sharron Bassano and
Mary Ann Christison**

> The teacher is no longer the only one who teaches. The students, while being taught, also teach. They become jointly responsible for a process in which all grow.
>
> **Paolo Freiere**
> *Pedagogy of the Oppressed*

Alta Book Center, Publishers

© 1995 by Alta Book Center, Publishers
San Francisco, California 94010

Printed in the United States of America

ISBN 1-882483-30-8

Dedication

This book is dedicated to our patient, courageous students, past and present, who have allowed us to learn our craft as they were learning language. And to *your* fortunate students, who have a teacher who cares about giving them the best one has to offer.

Acknowledgments

Thank you to language teachers everywhere! Over the last 17 years we have attended dozens of conferences, conventions, and workshops. We have enthusiastically shared successes and moaned over failures with hundreds of language teachers for a combined 32 years. Where do all the ideas in this book come from? As far as we know, they are original or from the "ethers" of the language teaching profession and amenable to being shared. If, however, you find something here that definitely belongs to someone else, or an idea or strategy originated by you, we would be delighted and relieved to know. We will gladly give credit where credit is due!

We would also like to acknowledge our editor, Chérie Lenz-Hackett, for her wonderful ideas, patience, tireless energy, and consistency.

Finally, thank you to Aarón Berman, Simón Almendares, and the wonderful people at Alta Book Center, Publishers who have believed in this project.

Project Editor	Aarón Berman, Alta Book Center
Content Editor	Chérie Lenz-Hackett, University of Washington
Design / Production	Cleve Gallat, CTA Graphics, San Francisco
Cover Art	Katherine Tillotson
Teacher Art	Sharron Bassano
Special Art	Joe Frazier, Illustrator, pages 101 and 120

Special Thanks to King Features Syndicate and
Matsushita Consumer Electronics Company

Introduction

✦ *col · lab · o · rate \v\ to work jointly with others in an intellectual endeavor; to cooperate with or willingly assist.*

✦ *cen · ter \n\ a person that is most important or pivotal in relation to an indicated activity, interest or condition; a source from which something originates.*

This book is written for secondary and adult education language teachers who:

1. believe that students want to and can take a more active and equal role in their learning process,

2. want to know how to help their students associate and work together willingly and skillfully for the mutual benefit of all concerned, and

3. would like to focus their lessons more on the needs, concerns, values, and interests of their students and less on the material presented in textbooks.

Chapter One offers a rationale for developing a student-centered, collaborative language classroom, outlining some of the major pedagogical, social, and personal advantages.

Chapter Two details many possible problems which may arise when attempting to initiate this sort of environment and offers suggestions for avoiding or working with student resistance.

Chapter Three offers concrete strategies that allow and encourage student initiative in daily classroom procedure and process, such as peer tutoring, progress monitoring, selection of content and materials preparation. These strategies not only build real language skills in context but give students more responsibility for their learning environment.

Chapter Four helps you to monitor your own progress in implementing a student-centered, collaborative classroom and gives suggestions for involving students in evaluation of their class.

Chapter Five presents scores of "generic" language acquisition group activities that may be used on an on-going basis.

Finally, we offer a bibliography of resources that either gives you more background, more ideas for process or more concrete, practical strategies.

☞ Important Advice

As long-time, experienced language teachers, we know it is very tempting to glance through a new resource book, peruse the table of contents, and immediately "cut to the chase." We skip over the first few chapters and go directly to the "activity section" looking for what to do on Monday morning. This works sometimes.

However, we assure you that this technique will not work with this resource. If you decide to ignore the first two chapters, we cannot guarantee that you will be able to successfully implement any of the practical strategies presented in the remainder of the book.

Without having a strong personal commitment for a philosophical change, without being able to anticipate the stumbling blocks, without knowing how to build students' group skills and enthusiasm step by step ahead of time, you may be in for a rude surprise! We promise we have cut out all the "baloney" and given you here only the most important information to enhance your venture into a more collaborative approach to language teaching. We encourage you to start at the beginning!

A revolution against those forms of privilege and power, which are based on claims to professional knowledge, must start with a transformation of consciousness about the nature of learning. This means, above all, a shift of responsibility for teaching and learning. Knowledge can be defined as a commodity only as long as it is viewed as the result of institutional objectives. Only when man recovers a sense of personal responsibility for what he learns and teaches can this spell be broken and the alienation of learning from living be overcome.

Ivan Illich
Deschooling Society

Table of Contents

Chapter 1

A COMPARISON OF APPROACHES

✦ *What are the major areas of teacher responsibility in a traditional, teacher-centered language classroom?*

✦ *What are the pedagogical, social, and personal advantages of sharing some of these responsibilities with your students?*

The traditional teacher-centered language classroom

In a traditional, teacher-centered language classroom there are six major areas of teacher responsibility. The language teacher:

1. establishes goals for the learners.

2. dispenses linguistic and cultural information.

3. initiates, organizes, and conducts practice.

4. assumes responsibility for motivating the students.

5. monitors progress and evaluates achievement.

6. enhances and maintains the learning environment.

Role 1

Learning goals and objectives are usually developed by teachers on the basis of what they regard as indispensable linguistic or cultural information for the learners. These goals are usually applied to all the learners in the classroom alike regardless of what each individual may need, desire or perceive as relevant. Not only do we decide what the language goals will be, but we define the course content and set up the progressions. We decide what is to be studied, in what order, with which materials, and according to standardized, accepted curricula. All these aspects are in turn tempered with our own personal educational philosophies, teaching styles, and preferred approaches and techniques.

Role 2

Language teachers traditionally are the dispensers of linguistic and cultural information. The student is the "empty vessel" waiting to be filled by the expert. We ask questions to which we already know the answers, and often before allowing learners the time to respond, we give them the answers to memorize!

Our peculiar western teaching system has conditioned us to believe that if we carefully define a thing, our learners will understand it. Language students are seldom asked to practice real acts of cognition, acts that require higher order thinking skills such as brainstorming, synthesizing ideas, problem solving, determining causes and effects, or considering alternatives and possible consequences. We teachers, by tradition, spend many classroom hours defining and dispensing language through endless teacher-initiated and teacher-led drills and exercises.

Role 3

Classroom management is also a realm traditionally governed solely by the teacher. It would seem that only teachers have the expertise to initiate, organize, and conduct language practice. We decide whether the students will work individually, in pairs, or in groups and whether the whole class is repeating in chorus, reciting individually, or allowed to speak at all. These decisions are dependent on the amount of credibility we give to one theory of learning over another or the confidence we place in a particular method. Often we make classroom management choices based on what is typical, standard, or required by the school.

Role 4

A fourth area of teacher responsibility is that of motivating the learners. We try to serve as personal examples of enthusiasm for the course content and instill interest in the course. We feel personally responsible for creating an environment in the classroom that is conducive to exploration of and involvement with the new language. Experienced teachers are well aware of the critical need for constant external motivation of the learners. Moving the student who is not intrinsically motivated is one of our most challenging tasks.

Role 5

Monitoring progress and evaluating achievement are also the property of the teacher in traditional language learning settings. As monitors, we break down the ultimate goal of the class experience into weekly, daily, and hourly objectives. We determine when the objectives should be reached, at what times, and at what pace. We are rarely able to take into consideration the "availability" of the individual learner–his or her mental, emotional or physical state at any particular time in the classroom. The course simply begins and ends at certain specified times, the exams are set on the same date for everyone regardless of the fatigues, preoccupations, or current concerns individual students may have at that moment.

As evaluators, teachers measure learners by their achievement of objectives in comparison with other learners in the classroom, or by some standardized measure. We continually ask students to perform so that we can tell them how they are doing. It is, in fact, an external evaluation, but most learners probably feel they have been "personally" evaluated along with the evaluation of their language skills.

Role 6

Students rarely take part in the organization and maintenance of the classroom environment. It is traditionally the teachers' "job" to see that desks are in order, windows are open, equipment is functioning, films are rewound, books are put back on the shelves, pencils are available, plants are watered, bulletin boards are decorated, etc. etc. No wonder we leave class feeling so exhausted...!

Each of these six teacher functions indicates the centrality of the teacher. Each function is expected by the students in the traditional language classroom setting. The teacher actively prepares, directs and gives; the learners passively receive, memorize, and take tests.

Though the teacher-centered classroom is the most common and accepted kind of classroom in second and foreign language instruction, it does have its well-known drawbacks. For example, attempting to conduct large, heterogeneous groups of students through any language program as one unit, obligates all students to cover the same amount of material, at the same rate, by the same method, and with the same material. This practice cannot take into consideration differences among learners such as aptitude, attitude, motivation, experience, age, learning styles, and educational background.

Moreover, while most choral work is in progress, some individuals may be lost two phrases behind the chorus or tuned out. Even well-experienced teachers who are gifted enough to move briskly and meaningfully from one language practice activity to another with a minimum of "choreography" problems must still hold the attention of a large number of learners simultaneously for long periods. Usually this sort of classroom strategy limits individual oral production to isolated sentences in answer to the teacher's questions or to specially fabricated, bite-sized utterances read aloud from a text.

Now that we have reminded you of everything you already know and have made sure we are on the same wave-length of assumptions, let's get down to business.

Why share some of this responsibility with your students?

It is the purpose of this guide to show you how to put more power and responsibility into the hands of the students—to give them a classroom environment where they are allowed the opportunity to participate in goal setting, classroom management, materials preparation, tutoring, environment enhancement, self-monitoring, and evaluation. We hope to offer a strong rationale and plenty of concrete strategies to convince you to develop your students' initiative, motivation, and group social skills concurrent with their second language.

Classroom experience and many research studies have shown that there are important pedagogical, social, and personal benefits to be derived from shifting to a decidedly student-centered, collaborative, language classroom where learning is a responsibility shared by students and teacher. (McGroarty, 1992; Kagan, 1986; DeAvila, Duncan, Navarrete, 1987; Cohen, 1986; Johnson and Johnson, 1987; Christison, 1988.)

Pedagogical advantages

When students begin to take a more active part in designing and conducting their language study—when they become more actively involved not only in practicing with and tutoring each other but in the very arrangement of the classroom and preparation of materials teachers have more time to work with individual students. Through careful and varied grouping of students (more about this in Chapter Three), teachers are much more able to deal with a large class size and dissimilar interests and proficiencies among learners—both obstacles and frustrations shared by nearly all classroom teachers as they try to reach each individual learner.

One of the main pedagogical advantages to developing a more student-centered, cooperative classroom is the opportunity for active oral participation of large numbers of students all at one time. In a classroom that features mostly teacher-led activity, we traditionally 1.) interact with only one student at a time while others listen and observe, or 2.) ask students to respond in chorus or small groups. Interaction among the learners themselves may be limited to reading dialogs or carrying out text-book "question-answer" exercises or substitution drills.

Students who are allowed to work in small groups, independently of the teacher, obviously have much more opportunity to practice real language in context. Structured group activities also lend themselves more readily to critical thinking, problem solving, and collaborative social skills development.

Current theories in second language acquisition suggest that communicative competence in a second language more readily and effectively develops when learners are exposed to and engaged in meaningful communication in that language. (Long and Porter, 1985; Swain, 1985; Kagan, 1986; Gaies, 1985; Long, 1981; Bejarano, 1987; Krashen and Terrell, 1983.) This meaningful activity can be interaction with written text or interaction in oral communication.

The important factor, if language is to be retained, is that the communication is intrinsically interesting and important to the learner. Collaborative language learning activities, both in and out of class, can help give the learner this kind of meaningful interaction in a full range of real and realistic situations or social settings.

Social advantages

Through meaningful tasks completed cooperatively with peers, students are allowed to rebuild their social skills in their new language, such as knowing how to interrupt politely and effectively, how to successfully negotiate meaning, how to disagree tactfully, and how to come to a compromise.

In a classroom centered upon themselves, students learn about each other–about different cultural or social values, opinions, beliefs. Through this interchange they may become more accepting, more tolerant, and appreciative of other races, religions, and ethnic groups. Conversely, they are able to share who they are and what they are interested in and concerned about with others from very different backgrounds but, perhaps, very similar current situations.

Students who carry out tasks that require listening to others, sharing ideas, information, opinions, and who are placed in a position of being somewhat dependent upon each other to succeed, develop empathy. They learn to like each other more and form communities. This interdependence does not happen as readily in a classroom that is highly teacher-centered, where students work essentially alone and in competition with each other.

During small group language tasks, learners have the opportunity to teach others, thereby solidifying their own learning. Giving new information to someone else is the best way for more verbal learners to retain information. It is also an excellent way to clarify what one knows, to bring bits and pieces together so that the information may be better used in more personalized ways.

After the initial "shock" of a change in classroom procedures, policies and expectations, most language learners enjoy working with their peers and are much more motivated by it than by standard audio-lingual or grammar exercises.

Personal advantages

Learners participating in a student-centered classroom which features a wide variety of collaborative group activity, are given the opportunity to develop self-discipline and accountability. Students who are allowed to expand their personal initiative and responsibility in the learning process, experience high self-confidence and greater self-esteem, a feeling of personal achievement, and they learn how to assess their own effort and their own work. Through self-chosen content, they actively learn to clarify their personal values, to say what they think and to proudly state their opinions in the second language.

Changing your classroom environment to one that is more conducted by and centered on the students themselves holds definite pedagogical, social, and personal advantages for both teacher and learners. (See bibliography for corroborating studies, articles, and texts. We didn't invent this stuff!)

In Chapter Two, we will examine ways in which to begin making a successful transition. We will discuss some of the normal, predictable problems that may arise initially for both teacher and students and share some suggestions on how to avoid or deal with them.

Chapter 2

Moving Toward Student-Centrality

✦ *How does the role of teacher change in a student-centered, collaborative classroom? The students' roles?*

✦ *How do you initiate the student-centered, collaborative classroom?*

✦ *What sort of resistance are you likely to encounter at first?*

✦ *Why?*

✦ *How can these stumbling blocks be avoided or dealt with?*

✦ *What are some essential skills for students to have in order to carry out group work effectively?*

The changing roles of the teacher and students

In traditional teacher-centered language classrooms, as we outlined in Chapter One, it is the teacher's responsibility to promote creative and stimulating activity in an environment that is conducive to learning. In a student-centered, collaborative classroom, teachers don't surrender these responsibilities, but rather encourage learners to become partners in the process. Sharing classroom responsibility and learning to work as a team, as you might suspect, require that both you and the learners modify personal views about the relationship between teaching and learning. In the same way that learners must drop stereotypical notions and expectations about what a classroom environment entails, teachers, too, must make a shift and let go of preconceived ideas about the role of the teacher. This does not happen magically. It is first a result of building a firm resolve on the parts of all concerned and then practicing step by step.

We teachers have been accustomed to presiding over a class; it is hard to step back and relinquish centrality. Arranging students into small groups and giving them a shared task to help them master the mechanics of language is easy. What is difficult is actually letting these groups function without us! It takes practice to circulate unobtrusively about the room, to move from group to group, assisting without interfering in their attempts at collaboration. It takes discipline not to jump in suddenly with a correction, a right answer or unsolicited "peace-keeping." At first it is hard to know when to intervene in an activity or when it would be best not to interrupt because the students are progressing well enough on their own. Students, too, need time to become accustomed to letting go their reliance on constant teacher intervention and direction. Through the collaborative tasks the teacher thoughtfully structures for the groups, students learn to carry out real-world functions in their new language. They begin to consult and confer with each other, to offer help, to ask for clarification, to rely on and trust their peers. Both language and interpersonal skills grow. Eventually, whenever teacher intervention does occur, it is undertaken so subtly that the learners sense no interruption of their activity.

Of course, teachers cannot just talk about the wonders of a collaborative, shared learning process. Rather we must demonstrate collaborative principles in actions that consistently and congruently guide, stimulate, encourage, and support student efforts at self-direction. We must let our democratic goals shine consistently upon all facets of classroom activity, not only in specific language-learning activity, but throughout the entire classroom experiences so that students become fully convinced of their equal partnership in the learning process.

It is sometimes assumed that an increase in learner initiative requires a reduction in the amount of control a teacher exercises. On the contrary, it is not only *possible* for a teacher to retain complete control of the classroom while students exercise most of the initiative, it is *imperative*. Teacher control, or structure, as we prefer to call it, enhances student initiative and responsibility rather than thwarts it. Structure is essential; students need a framework within which to interact. You provide that framework–the rules or guides–that assists students to carry on confidently and successfully as a group.

In a shared classroom the teacher is the source of linguistic and cultural information. But the teacher is also the accountable authority who:

1. helps develop and discover meaningful task oriented-activities that truly engage the students and motivate them to conduct themselves productively;

2. strives to involve the students in the process as fully as possible;

3. promotes a strong, congenial interaction among individual students and between students and teacher; and

4. has an ultimate goal of allowing the dichotomy of teacher-student to disappear and promotes the emergence of partners in a collaborative venture, each one being both a teacher and a learner.

Before initiating any reorganization of your classroom, please know that self-direction and collaboration are not innate behaviors; they are skills that can be learned. They are potential capacities that humans have that can be developed but only through strong commitment on the part of all concerned, carefully sequenced guidelines and strategies, and continual reminders of goals. And it is a rather slow process.

In Chapters Three and Four you will find specific guidelines and activities that allow students to become more involved in directing their learning experience and in working in collaborative, self-directed groups.

☞ A reminder: None of the ideas you will find in Chapters Three, Four and Five are guaranteed to be successful unless you have a firm grasp on the information on the following pages. Please read carefully. If you skip over these pages, going right on into activities, you may find the results unsettling. You need keys to open this door.

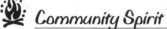

Initiating the collaborative classroom experience

Problems can (and often do) arise when students begin to make the transition from more traditional classroom procedures. It is generally recognized that how one feels about learning can affect one's ability to learn. One of the strongest factors to influence achievement specifically in the language classroom is a feeling of anxiety. This emotional reaction can be a result of many social, cultural, and personal factors (which, of course, you, personally, may have little influence over). But it is also often produced by encounters with unfamiliar instructional practices.

It is very likely that students in your language class will not be adequately prepared for a collaborative classroom experience and without careful initiation may exhibit frustration, confusion, anger, resentment, or other unsettling responses. These feelings can manifest themselves in many forms of unproductive behavior in the language classroom. But take heart! We have identified for you (based on past experiences!) some of the more common possibilities. Recognition of these as behaviors with logical roots can be a valuable lesson in moving toward resolution and progress.

Following this outline, we will offer a few guesses as to the causes of these reactions, and then discuss essential planning that will help you avoid or deal with student disorientation and resistance - concepts that are invaluable to successful implementation of collaborative, student-centered language learning environments.

Possible initial reactions of students who are unprepared for collaborative classrooms

Aggression

Discussion may be dominated and controlled by a few learners who are in disagreement no matter what issue arises. Except for a few vocal extroverts, most of the group members may seem to lose interest in the task or conversation and let someone else take over.

Withdrawal

A few learners may appear shy or embarrassed. Their heads may be buried in dictionaries. They might smile nervously, perspire profusely, squirm in their chairs, remain silent, and in general, avoid participation. They may begin working on homework from some other class, ignoring your assignment.

Apathy

Discussion of ideas may not be carried out. Learners may seem to care little about what is going on in the group. No one seems willing to do the work at hand. Some learners may gaze out the window or put their heads down on the desk.

Evasion

Learners may talk about anything but the assigned task, often using their primary language. No one seems able to get started.

Egocentrism

Each learner may have his or her own idea about what is correct or best. They may talk past each other, with no one really listening or seem interested only in making their own points.

Condescension

Learners may act overly friendly and polite, reaching agreement easily but not expressing any real feelings or opinions. Learners may be only superficially engaged and complete the assignment in a fraction of the time you have anticipated.

Complaints

Ideas, topics, tasks or other group members may be flatly rejected. Students may complain about not having enough time or enough guidance. Negative comments may be made about other group members or about the assignment, possibly causing you to become defensive. Alienation may seem to increase.

"Disorderly conduct"

Finally, students may even throw things, begin to push, tease or flirt. They may start to scribble on the materials or crinkle them up. They may leave their groups, wander about and get off task, sharpen pencils, or make strange noises. Walkmans may be plugged into ears. Chaos ensues. (Yes, even adults do this!)

Why do students react this way?

As we admitted earlier, each of these examples has come from many years of trial and error teaching. Not being sociologists or psychologists, we can only guess at what causes these student reactions to the unfamiliar, student-centered, collaborative environment. But we believe that most problems can be dealt with by forethought and planning. Read through the following abbreviated list. How many of these factors which may cause group work to fail are something you, the teacher, could anticipate, counteract, and plan for?

Our students may have:

✦ low self-esteem or low self-confidence

✦ short attention spans

✦ very different expectations

✦ physical, emotional, family, or economic problems

✦ prejudices (ethnic, racial, gender, age)

✦ shy or aggressive personalities

✦ not enough second language skill to carry out assigned task

✦ no experience at group work

✦ no real intrinsic motivation

Maybe the teacher:

✦ gave unclear instruction

✦ did not provide a rationale

✦ chose a topic that was uninteresting, irrelevant, or unfamiliar

✦ had unrealistic expectations regarding product or process and allowed too much or not enough time

✦ expected strangers to work together as trusting friends

We have been able to successfully predict and counteract most of the above. Rarely have we given up on a group of students and limited ourselves to strictly teacher-centered methods. To help you and your students escape these disasters and save you the time of "reinventing the wheel," we offer the following essential preparatory guidelines for you to consider well in advance of experimenting with the actual concrete strategies in this book (or, indeed, strategies in any other resource books that feature collaborative, second-language acquisition tasks!)

How can we prepare students for collaborative group work?

Before students can work successfully in groups, they need to be prepared for the collaborative experience. The stage must be set. In brief, we can help prepare our students by doing the following things:

1. Gain knowledge of the students' past schooling experience to determine their expectations.

2. In the beginning, give them exactly what they expect. Validate their past experience by beginning with the familiar.

3. Communicate your personal expertise from the very first moment of class–your experience, your competence, the success your past students have had.

4. Get acquainted with your students. Allow them to get acquainted with each other. Strangers have a difficult time collaborating!

5. Learn about your students' values, interests, concerns, and goals so that when the group work begins, the content can be made as relevant as possible.

6. Build a strong awareness of why group skills are so important in learning a second language. Put up posters, for example, that affirm how strongly you believe in supportive group effort in the classroom. Try to get them on your side by helping them understand all the benefits of becoming a productive, active group member.

7. Gradually implement change. Give students time to build the necessary skills and motivation so that they may more easily adopt the process as their own.

8. Offer choices for solitary tasks for those few students who are initially highly resistant to group activity. Forcing participation of the reluctant ones serves no pedagogical purpose.

Now, here are a few more details on the above eight points. You can become more aware of students' previous classroom experience by conducting a classroom survey or open discussion. We need more information about students before deciding where to begin. In what kinds of activities have they participated in other classes? What did they like best? What was the most difficult part? What was helpful? What was not helpful? What was most satisfying? How did they relate to their previous teachers? How were they treated? How and when were they corrected? What sorts of assignments did they carry out outside of class? Do they expect to succeed or fail now?

Encouraging learners to tell about their initiation to language learning puts both you and the learners in immediate touch with the positive and negative aspects of early training. It allows them the opportunity to assume the role of teacher and of someone with something important to share. It indicates an openness, interest, and sincerity on the part of the instructor to plan an experience that suits them well. It lessens the feeling among the students that their background is unknown or irrelevant.

When learners talk about aspects of their previous language experiences that they didn't like or didn't find helpful, they almost always choose to try something different, something that might work better for them. Curiosity is a strong motivator. If you can arrange to have your students ask to try something that you suggest may be more effective, their resistance will naturally be lowered.

There are several risks involved in opening up the class for discussion of classroom practice. The teacher needs to possess a great deal of self-assurance. It is absolutely essential that we communicate our professionalism and expertise to the learners. We must be strong, competent, self-confident models. Most learners, conditioned by past formal educational experience, desperately crave leadership and structure. They want freedom of choice, but they also want and deserve the feeling of stability and guidance. They want to know that the classroom responsibility they are being given is given to them purposely by a proficient, well-trained instructor, not by one who simply may not have leadership ability.

In order to build confidence, teachers must know why they do what they do, and how to do it well. We must be convinced that the approach we use is helpful to rapid language gain. Learners know when we are unsure or tentative, and they can lose confidence very quickly. Confidence, once lost, is very difficult to regain.

Learners want to understand why they are being asked to participate in certain unfamiliar (or even bizarre, according to their model of the educational world) classroom practices. Adult learners, especially, often have difficulty at first with what appears to be game-playing. They have immediate goals and feel they have no time to waste. Some subconsciously believe that if they are having fun, if they are interested and enjoying themselves, they must not be learning anything. They crave a good solid assurance from the teacher about the viability of particular activities. If you are not entirely sure of the rationale behind what you want to do and your ability to clarify it to your students, it is better not to try it.

There is much persuasive power in positive, instant feedback and visible progress in each class hour, no matter how small. Encourage your learners. Show them evidence of successful performance and achievement with increasingly more challenging, complex, or sustained tasks. If students can be shown any sort of immediate result for their efforts, a new idea will sell itself.

In order to further ensure that learners approach their new language class in the right frame of mind, teachers must begin slowly and plan for a gradual restructuring process. We will first offer our students "Learning with a capital L" which is anything they are accustomed to and expect. Slowly and subtlety we introduce new methods and materials with the learners' enthusiastic permission, starting where they are, and moving them slowly to a place that is likely to be more effective. Change cannot take place overnight; cooperative skills must be practiced over a long period of time step-by-step. Continue to offer choices to the few extra-resistant hold-outs. They will come around. We have found that rarely will individuals choose to continue working alone, separating themselves from the group for very long when they see friendly, supportive, entertaining activity transpiring all around them.

Just as we must be aware of where our students have been, we also need to find out where they are going. Surely it is plain to all of us that the most effective lessons and the most motivating are those that reach out to the perceptual world of the learner and validate that world. If our lesson content points to their needs, their purposes, their interests, then our lesson process becomes less obtrusive. When our learners are aware that what they experience, feel, think, plan is worth sharing with others, they will be less reluctant.

Finally, if we hope to lower a learner's resistance to change and promote adjustment to the new classroom, we must also attend to the development of group trust. If our classrooms become islands of security and support, no one will be afraid of ridicule or embarrassment. If our students feel uncomfortable with other class members, will they be able to achieve the freedom that is necessary for risk-taking? Probably not.

Building group skills over time

There are four stages in the development of group skills.

1. Learners develop an awareness that collaborative learning exists and gain an understanding of its importance and efficacy.

2. Learners begin to understand what some of the necessary skills are to be an effective group member.

3. Learners begin to practice the words and skills in a somewhat self-conscious, mechanical (and often awkward) manner. This is akin to learning to drive a car and is often the most difficult step.

4. After a good deal of practice, they will gain an unconscious, automatic use of collaborative skills both in class and, we hope, out of class.

What, specifically, are some of the necessary skills that learners must have to work effectively in groups?

Students should ultimately be able to:

1. Form their groups quickly without disturbing others.

2. Stay with the assigned group and work with the people in that group for a short time.

3. Participate with somewhat muted voices when several groups are working in the room.

4. Establish turn-taking patterns and determine each group member's role, such as time-keeper, secretary, English monitor, reader, reporter, encourager, etc.

5. Use each other's names.

6. Look at and listen actively to each speaker in the group.

7. Avoid "put-down" or argumentative behavior.

8. Clarify assignments with the teacher and other group members if necessary.

9. Watch time limit for each individual or each activity and remind each other to stay on task.

10. Express support of other members in their group.

11. Listen and draw out ideas from more hesitant members.

12. Offer to explain, clarify, summarize, or assist.

13. Correct or add to information or ideas for other group members in a polite, supportive way.

14. Criticize ideas rather than people.

15. Ask for explanation or rationalization for answers or conclusions given by other members of their group.

To help facilitate the transition into a more collaborative classroom, we have found it helpful to prepare various posters to refer to on a regular basis. These posters remind students of the value of group work, the necessary basic skills, the kind of language that is helpful, etc. Of course, the posters you design will have to match the age, language proficiency and sophistication of your learners, but here are just some samples.

GROUP SKILLS

Please:

form your groups quickly

stay with your group

remember to use soft voices

Choose to be:

language monitor

task monitor

time-keeper

secretary

clarifier

encourager

reporter

**WORKING IN GROUPS
GIVES US THE OPPORTUNITY TO:
PRACTICE SPEAKING
PRACTICE LISTENING
LEARN ABOUT EACH OTHER
LEARN NEW IDEAS
GIVE HELP
ASK FOR HELP
SHARE INFORMATION
PRACTICE NEGOTIATING
PRACTICE COMPROMISING
BE LEADERS
BE FOLLOWERS
CREATE THINGS TOGETHER
BE SUCCESSFUL TOGETHER
LEARN DEMOCRATIC PROCESS**

**EFFECTIVE GROUP MEMBERS:
USE THEIR PARTNERS' NAMES
LOOK AND LISTEN TO EACH OTHER
TAKE TURNS...GIVE OTHERS A TURN
OFFER THEIR HELP
ARE POLITE:
MAKE NO PUT-DOWN NOISES!
SMILE!**

Lower level students will need some special assistance in carrying out group tasks successfully. They not only need clear, concise, well-modeled demonstrations as to how to carry out the task, but it has to be made very clear to them what is expected as a product, how long they have to work, who should go first, what the procedure is, what the goal is, etc.

Lower level students also profit by pre-practicing some essential phrases that keep group work going. These sorts of phrases need to be pre-taught and practiced. We also suggest that a poster be made so that students can review these kinds of phrases before each group task.

Thank you for reading all of Chapters One and Two before going on to the practical strategies. This tells us you are not just browsing for a "quick fix" sort of activity, but rather you are looking to make a well-planned, thoughtful change in the entire philosophy that governs your classroom. We commend you for your commitment.

Phrases We Can Use:

I don't understand.

What did you say?

Excuse me?

Speak more slowly please.

Do you need help?

Show me/him/her.

Let me see it.

Are you finished?

Quickly! We have four minutes.

Just a minute.

I need help.

It's your/my/his/her turn.

You first, then me.

Okay?

Chapter 3

THE DAILY ROUTINE

✦ *What kinds of specific classroom responsibilities can be shared by both students and teacher?*

✦ *What are some concrete strategies you can use right away that both facilitate the average classroom day and give opportunity for building real communication skills in the second-language?*

Responsibilities students and teachers can share

The possibilities for shared activity in the language classroom are innumerable. In Chapter Five, you will learn many different basic collaborative activities that specifically focus on language practice. But, first of all, in this chapter we will offer concrete strategies for student involvement in more "process oriented" activities. Though these activities provide an effective natural context for building real language skills, the focus is on the general nuts and bolts of the daily classroom routine. Two major benefits in one! These activities include:

1. daily classroom environment and social tasks

2. peer tutoring

3. revision of writing

4. selection of content and determining objectives

5. materials preparation, and

6. progress monitoring and evaluation

Classroom environment and social tasks

This, we find, is the easiest area in which to begin. From day one, we have found students to be very willing and capable of taking responsibility for many of the following standard, day-to-day classroom needs:

1. room arrangement

2. keeping attendance

3. welcoming, introducing, registering, orienting new students

4. planning parties, potlucks, outings

5. maintaining student folders and charts

6. decorating bulletin boards and the rest of the classroom

7. planning for field trips and classroom visitors

8. advising on disciplinary action, cultural and personal misunderstandings, or other critical incidents that transpire in the classroom

9. selling books, notebooks, pencils

10. managing the coffee break (shopping and sales)

11. caring for the plants

12. putting the chairs in order after school

13. cleaning blackboards, emptying waste basket, general putting away of things after class

14. setting up for films, videos, slide presentations

15. caring for equipment

16. setting up and managing classroom check-out library

17. building shelves, room dividers, learning stations

18. maintaining a storage system for certain materials

19. handing out materials, books, scissors, rulers, crayons, etc.

20. making announcements

21. calling students back in from break time

22. phoning absentee students

Each class of course has its own particular environmental and social tasks according to age level and type of program. Try posting a sign-up list and asking pairs of students to volunteer for certain tasks. (Pairs, just in case one is absent.) Usually you only have to point out a need, get the volunteers organized, and express your confidence in them. In this way, students not only move a little further down the road for taking responsibility for their learning environment and their classmates, but also save you a couple hours each day of uninspiring yet necessary work.

Peer tutoring

Peer tutoring refers to any activity where students help each other to understand, review, practice, or remember. The first hurdle is to get past the notion that helping is cheating. In our classroom, knowing something and *not* sharing it with others is cheating! Hang large charts in your room, perhaps, that say such things as "Give some help!" or "Ask for help!" or "We learn more quickly if we help each other!"

Peer tutoring provides opportunity for students to speak more in their new language and to learn by teaching. It is a process of collaboration, of pooling knowledge in order to solve a problem or complete a task. It may assume any one of the following things:

1. One student has more information than another.

2. Each student has some information which the other may not have.

3.   Both students have equal prior information but apply that information with different insights.

4.   Both have equal prior information but work at different rates.

This collaboration includes mutual cognitive and affective support for one another; it is a process which may be very therapeutic especially for newcomers who may be sharing the same difficulties. Peer tutors often develop friendships which carry over to out-of-class time. Following are strategies for utilizing the idea of peer tutoring.

Tutoring Strategy 1   **Relay**

Teach some grammar item or subject matter to four students (while others work on a separate reading or writing task). Send these four students over to sit down with four other students to teach them what they have just learned. You now have eight tutors who can go over to eight more students and teach them. Carry on until all students in the class are somewhat familiar with the lesson. Then form groups of five or six. Hand out a "test" or question sheet based on the subject matter or grammar item on which they have been tutoring each other. Have them work together to complete the task as a group.

Tutoring Strategy 2   **Group Memory**

In groups of six, give the students a line or a short dialog to practice and memorize. Set a time limit. Each group member will receive extra credit if everyone in his or her group can say the line or carry out the dialog from memory when time is up. (When it comes down to doing it, they can whisper prompts to each other if necessary; it's just an extension of the tutoring effort!)

Tutoring Strategy 3   **Each and Every**

Hand out a discrete point question sheet–the "one-right-answer" variety. Working in small groups, each student must complete the worksheet correctly (or no one in the group gets to go home!). The first person in a group to complete the work comes to you to check its accuracy. When the paper is correct, that student goes back to the group and makes sure that everyone in the group is on the right track and offers assistance if requested. Any group member may assist but may not actually do the writing for any other student.

All sheets are checked carefully by the group for accuracy before stapling them together and handing them in. You will review only one of the worksheets from each group at random. All students in a group will receive the same number of points as the one you review.

Tutoring Strategy 4   **Test Me**

Students work in pairs with discrete point worksheets. Partner A has a copy with blanks to fill in, multiple choice, or sentences to transform in some way. Partner B has a copy of the completed work sheet. Partner A reads aloud, working through the exercise orally. Partner B acts as a tester for the student, advising him or her if the response is correct or not and prompting if necessary. When they are finished, another set of complete-incomplete worksheets is passed out and students switch roles.

Tutoring Strategy 5   **Listen Please**

This paired activity focuses on listening and pronunciation. Student A has a set of picture cards placed on the table in front of him or her. Student B has a set of sentence cards corresponding to the pictures. Student B reads the sentence cards one at a time. Student A picks up the corresponding picture. If it is a correct match, Student B hands over the sentence card. Continue until all cards are gone, then switch roles. You may use any sort of pictures cut from duplicatable picture resources, your texts, or magazines. You may focus on concrete vocabulary or on specific sounds or phonics areas that students find particularly challenging. While the actual practice may not help too much to improve a student's pronunciation, it at least builds an awareness of the importance of mastering certain English sounds. Some sample sentences might be, for example:

Her husband is a pilot.	Her husband is a pirate.
I thought about Mexico.	I taught about Mexico.
Collect the papers, please.	Correct the papers, please.
Eat the soup.	Heat the soup.

Tutoring Strategy 6   **Comparing Answers**

Readings prepared for language students often have a set of comprehension questions following the stories. After students have individually written answers to the questions, have them form groups of three or four to compare responses. When responses to any particular question differ, students try to explain why they answered the way they did. As students work, circulate among them to help point out any clues or missed information. The goal is for students to come to consensus (without coming to blows) on an appropriate response. Students may give more attention to their written responses if they know in advance that they will have to "justify" them.

Revision of writing

Students may also offer valuable tutoring assistance to one another in the way of revision of writing. The moment that students finish a writing assignment, motivation is at its highest. They want to know how they did; they want to know if they are readable or even close! Most teachers collect written work, take it home to "correct" (rewrite, edit, revise, make comments) and return it the following day or sometimes two days later. By then the students may have lost interest. They may glance over their work briefly to count the red lines and arrows and then throw it away. An important moment for the student has been lost, not to mention several teacher homework hours. There are many ways in which to provide that motivating instant feedback that students respond well to. Following are possibilities you may want to try.

Revision Strategy 1   **On the Board**

After teaching a specific grammar point to the class as a whole group, showing samples, rules for formation, and usage in context, give your students a set amount of time to compose several sentences that exemplify the structure. Have them compare papers with one another to see if they can find anything they think needs work. Tell students that if they are not absolutely sure about their examples, they can go to the board and write them. (You will not be taking their papers home.) Several students can go to the board at one time and write the sentences they are not sure of. When the board is full of student samples, you and the whole group discuss them together to see if anyone can offer suggestions for revision.

You might initially think that students would be too shy to write sentences they had doubts about on the board in front of everyone.

And you are right! At first they tend to write only sentences they know are correct. But they soon realize that no one individual is put on the spot, and if they don't take a risk, they will never know if they have understood or not. The group discussion that ensues as students attempt to analyze their work is phenomenal.

Revision Strategy 2   **Show Me Yours**

Peer revision of homework can be a very simple procedure. Groups of two or three students compare papers and discuss possible problem areas in their writing regarding tense, word choice, spelling, etc. You can move from group to group confirming their guesses, assisting where requested. This few minutes spent consulting with peers before turning in work gives them an excellent chance to reconsider the assignment and go over any areas of difficulty. It also provides real oral interaction focusing on a written assignment.

Revision Strategy 3   **Selective Edit**

Learning to check a composition for errors is not an easy task. Students must be given experience with editing techniques before they can be asked to revise their first drafts or respond to those of other students. Editing in pairs can be a very effective process using some of the following procedures.

1. Ask the students to look for only one or two kinds of errors in the composition, such as a clearly stated topic sentence. They can look for spelling and punctuation errors. Whatever you choose, be specific and ask the students to look for those things only.

2. Have one student read his/her first draft aloud to a partner while both look or listen for errors of the assigned type.

3. Students stop reading when they think they have spotted a problem. They discuss how to repair it and make a mutual decision for revising.

Revision Strategy 4   **Blue Pencil Collective**

When students have turned in a writing assignment, ask students to sit with a partner. Hand out one piece of writing to each pair (not their own work). You keep half of the papers to work on as the students are working. Instruct the students to look for specific kinds of problem areas (which you itemize). The pairs of students work together locating and circling the specific problem areas. They write their suggestions for revision on a piece of note paper and sign

their names to the suggestion sheet. Pairs that finish before others are given a second paper with which to work. Return the writing and the suggestion sheets to the writers of the work for consideration when doing a second draft.

Revision Strategy 5   **What's the Problem?**

Photocopy two or three short essays without the students' names on them. Hand them out to the entire class to revise and to work on as a whole group with you. Ask the group to look for specific things in the essays that might be examples of ideas already covered in the class lectures. Be sure to discuss the best parts of the writings as well, pointing out especially interesting phrases or choices of words. This activity is also very effectively done on an overhead projector with transparencies.

Selection of content areas and determining objectives

In many cases, learners come to class without clear or consistent goals other than a desire to learn another language. It is our task to help them sort out the confusion and give some sort of order to their effort. They may already know some of the essentials according to traditional curricula, but it is our job to guide the students to discover for themselves what is worth learning, worth doing, and worth knowing in their new language.

This is not to say that the goals of the school and the teacher are not considered; they are equally important insofar as they actually coincide with or become those of the students.

Although it often remains the property of the teacher as the language expert to determine the actual syllabus priorities in the classroom, the students can and should be the selectors of content especially related to topics of conversation, readings, and writing assignments. They should have a say in what parts of the culture they wish to explore.

In order to help them choose specific areas of exploration, begin making a list of possible alternatives on the board. Have them add their areas of interest to the list. Or ask them to work in groups to come up with 10 areas they would like to learn, talk, read, or write about. Have the whole group share their lists and vote to prioritize the five most interesting to begin with. For example, areas of conversation might include: sports, history, religion, politics, family, cultural differences, sciences, current news events, American geography, work and money, leisure time, romance, etc.

A beginning list of life skill areas for adult language situations might be: shopping, getting a driver's license, renting a house, applying for a job, speaking with the doctor, community services, employment training, etc.

Priorities for study should be set according to a specific set of criteria established by the students and teacher together. For example:

✦ Is it interesting? Informative? Entertaining?

✦ Is it valuable for the future?

✦ What sorts of resources can be found–people, readings, community agencies?

✦ Where could we go outside of class to learn more about the topic?

✦ Whom could we invite to speak to us?

✦ Does the teacher (or anyone else in the class) know anything about the subject?

After choosing a subject area with which to begin, find out what kinds of things they *already know* and what they *want to know* about the subject. Break the topic down into manageable subtopics. For example:

Dealing with Emergencies

1. Who to call for emergency assistance.

2. How to report an accident, a fire, a robbery, a poisoning, a medical emergency.

3. What first aid equipment and procedures to use.

4. How to prepare for earthquakes and what to do after one.

5. How to make our homes safer places for our children.

6. What emergency agencies such as police, fire department, highway patrol, ambulances, hospitals, poison control, etc. serve our community and how to work with them?

Following are five strategies for assisting students to make choices in the content of their lessons.

Content Selection Strategy 1 **Picture It**

Beginning level students can bring in objects or tear pictures from magazines that tell you what words or content areas they want to know about. You could also hang up pictures or signs around the room that depict places in the community where your students need to be able to speak English. As a whole class, have students go stand by the picture or sign that is the place of highest importance to them for speaking English. Continue moving about having them select a second and third choice. Make a tally so that they are aware of the class' democratic decision.

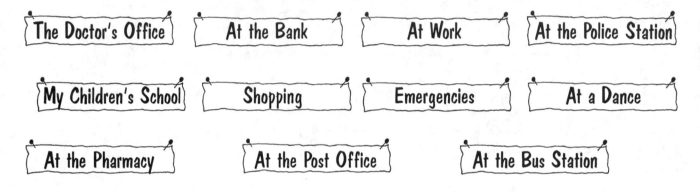

Content Selection Strategy 2 **Campaign**

Have your advanced students bring articles from newspapers or magazines that represent topics they would like to work with in English. Have them campaign to the class giving reasons why that topic would be a good area of exploration. After students have shared their suggestions, have them vote on the most preferred topic.

Content Selection Strategy 3
Voice a Choice

Bring in a page with several "rank order" choices on it related to different themes to spark interest. For example:

Have your students individually write numbers 1, 2, or 3 according to their first, second, and third choice for each of these questions and take turns discussing each of their choices in small groups.

As a homework assignment, ask each student to choose a topic of personal interest (family, employment, sports, music, technology, etc.) and create a rank order sheet similar to the one they just completed. The sheet should have four questions with three answer choices for each question. The teacher duplicates their pages for use in discussion groups over a period of time. Then students could vote on preferred topics from the sheets to focus on in depth during later classes.

VOICE YOUR CHOICE   Leisure Time

1. Where would you rather be on a Saturday afternoon?
   __ lying in the sun in the back yard
   __ shopping at a mall with $200 to spend
   __ playing racquet ball

2. What kind of evening would you prefer?
   __ quiet evening at home talking with two good friends
   __ going out dancing in a noisy club with ten friends
   __ going to a great movie alone

3. If you were in a music shop with $20, what would you buy?
   __ heavy metal rock music
   __ music from your native country
   __ Vivaldi and Mozart

4. Which do you prefer?
   __ playing sports   __ watching sports
   __ sleeping late

Content Selection Strategy 4   **Graffiti**

Hang large newsprint sheets on the walls around the room, each sheet having a conversation topic written as a heading - Leisure Time, Friendship and Love, Work and Money, America, Politics, TV and Movies, Travel, etc. Ask students to consider their personal favorite topic of those listed and go and stand by the chart to show their interest. (All students move at the same time.) You and your students can immediately see the balance of interests in the group. Then have them move and stand by a chart that represents a topic they never like to talk about. Third, give them each a crayon or watercolor marker and have them move about the room for about ten minutes just writing comments, or questions or drawing pictures on the charts. Give them time to go around and read the charts. This is a low-threatening way to get students to begin taking a personal stand—an excellent

INTEREST SURVEY

Please check the five most important things to you right now. Mark the most important number 1, the next most important, number 2, etc.

I need to improve my English right now to:

___ talk to my manager/boss

___ apply for work

___ read labels in the store

___ understand TV and movies

___ go to college

___ get my driver's license

___ talk to my doctor

___ read the newspaper

___ talk with my lawyer

___ order in a restaurant

___ write letters

___ find an apartment

activity for students who may be nervous about speaking. It is also a structured but energizing way to get them up and out of their seats for a short time, an important consideration in a long class period.

Content Selection Strategy 5
Surveys

Finally, regarding life skills or adult basic competencies for adult language learners, it is not difficult to do surveys of your group to find out their main concerns and interests. Adolescent and young adult language learners will eagerly respond to surveys about their hobbies, social interests, academic concerns, and career goals.

Students work alone to complete the survey. Then as a group they plot their responses on a graph or chart so that students are aware of the wide range of interests (or the similarity of interests) present in the classroom.

Materials preparation

The following strategies are designed to get students involved in the preparation of learning materials at several different language proficiency levels. In addition to providing a context for real language practice and reinforcement, materials prepared by students are another way to involve students in classroom process as well.

Materials Strategy 1   **Matched Sets**

Have two students at the beginning level work together to find vocabulary pictures in a magazine, cut them out, and paste them on 3 x 5 cards. When they have prepared fifteen or so, they make word cards that match the vocabulary pictures using colored pens and 3 x 5 index cards. This vocabulary may be selected at random by the students, or the teacher may provide a list of words for which they must find pictures. When they are finished, they clip their entire set together with a large paper clip or bind them in a rubber band.

These card sets may be used in three ways:

1. Pairs or small groups of students work together with one set of cards, to sort out and match up the pairs, and test each other on pronunciation.

2. Use as a "concentration" activity for the whole class. For this, you will need a large pocket board to put the cards in (available at any education supply house). Write large numbers on the backs of the cards, scramble the set, and place them in the pocket board number-side out. One student says two numbers, and the teacher turns the two cards around to see if they are a match. If they are, the cards are removed from the board and given to the student. If they are not, the cards are turned back around and replaced in their original position. Number calling continues until all matches have been made. (If you have no pocket board, sticking the cards to the blackboard with masking tape works almost as well.)

3. Half of the students, standing on one side of the room, get one picture each. The other half stand on the other side of the room and get one word card each. Set a timer. Give them four minutes to move about and find their partner and go stand by a wall with him or her, showing their matches. When all students are standing in a circle around the room with a partner, go quickly around the room, the whole group saying what the partners are holding.

For more advanced groups, ask them to make matched sets with pictures and sentences or pictures and paragraphs.

Materials Strategy 2   **Illustrate the Point**

Tell the students a story. Ask them what kinds of pictures could best illustrate the vocabulary, the actions, the people, or concepts in the story. Write some of their ideas on the board. Each student chooses one illustration to make. Give them a time limit to prepare their drawings (use construction paper and crayons). Have them tape their pictures to the board in the correct sequence. Have individuals take turns in small groups telling parts of the story according to the pictures. Or, collect the drawings, shuffle them, and hand them back out. Have students form a line putting the scrambled pictures in order. Then, each student down the line says something about his or her

picture so that the story is retold. Save the pictures to use again sometime when you tell the story to another group.

Materials Strategy 3   **Co-op Creations**

Form groups of four. Give each group a different magazine picture. Have them create a one-page story together about the picture (orally or in writing). Write a list of verbs or idioms ahead of time on the board. Ask them to use each of those words or ideas in their picture stories in any way they can. When time is up, each group will take turns coming to the front of the room to tell their story. They will be amazed that the vocabulary and idioms can be used in so many completely different contexts.

Materials Strategy 4   **On the Wall**

Ahead of time, write concrete nouns on small strips of paper and put them into a box. (For more advanced students, have them write concrete nouns of their choice on small strips of paper.) Each student pulls two strips from the box. On a long piece of butcher paper (5' or 6') taped to the wall, students will create a cooperative mural together illustrating all the words from the box. They may do this in one of two ways:

1. Read all of their words aloud to the class and decide together beforehand how they will proceed and what they will create, or

2. Just go to the paper as a whole group and begin working, trying to tie in their own drawings with someone else's and just see what happens. (I have the word "hat." He has the word "sheep." I will draw a hat on his sheep, etc.) When the mural is complete, shuffle all the strips of paper. Hand them out again at random. Students will write labels under the pictures according to the strip they now have. Keep the mural for study by another class.

Materials Strategy 5   **Mirror Image**

Hand out small mirrors—one to each student. Have students look into their mirrors and draw their own faces on pieces of large construction paper. Collect the pictures and mix them up. Then have them write a short "autobiography" without writing their name on their paper. (Give them a list of questions to answer, if they need the structure or ideas.) As they are writing, hang their self portraits on the wall. When time is up, collect the writings, shuffle them and hand them out at random. Students as a large group go to the self-portraits and try to attach the autobiography to its correct portrait. After students have confirmed their guesses, save the pictures. Many other uses for them will arise!

Materials Strategy 6   **Sentence Scrambles**

Hand out a stack of small card strips to each student (3 x 5s cut lengthwise into three strips each). Ask each student to look in the text at this week's unit of study and find one sentence of five words or more. It may be affirmative, negative or interrogative. Ask them to copy the sentence exactly as it appears including punctuation and capitalization - one word per card. Give them a time limit and ask them to write very carefully. (Others will have to read these cards.) Those who finish quickly can write a second sentence. Ask them to then scramble their words and paper clip them together. Collect all the sentences in a shoe box. Hand out one set to each pair of students to unscramble on their desk. As soon as they think they have it in the correct order, they check with you, and if they are correct, they scramble it up, clip it together, put it back in the box and take another. This activity can continue for fifteen minutes or more for maximum oral collaboration (as well as work with syntax). Students could also copy each sentence in their notebook as they finish forming it, if they need that sort of practice.

Materials Strategy 7   **Spontaneous Worksheet**

Advanced students can prepare study sheets for other class members, e.g., sentences with verb tense missing, multiple choice questions, fill-in-the-blanks, etc. Assign a time limit, circulate around the class offering assistance when requested. Some may write three examples, others may complete ten. When time is up, collect all the papers and ask each student to find a partner. Hand out the papers at random, one paper to each pair. (They should not have the study sheet they created.) Those partnerships who finish with their paper quickly may get another one to work on. Use peer revision strategies for checking the work.

Materials Strategy 8   **Speech! Speech!**

Assign advanced students to give short speeches on topics they are familiar with and interested in (something from the news, something about their country or a country of their choice, a recipe, something about their work, about how a particular thing works or what it is used for, how it is made, etc.) Ask them to prepare a quiz sheet about their speech. Students who listen to the speech must take

notes and ask for clarification if they do not understand what the speechmaker is saying. (This continual feed-back from the audience allows speakers to know exactly when they are or are not communicating.) This activity is valuable to the listener as well as the speaker. They listen actively, take notes, try to extract important information, and may begin to overcome their reticence to ask clarification questions. They know they will be held responsible for taking the quiz.

Student progress monitoring and evaluative tasks

Evaluation is much more than merely testing and assigning grades based on performance; it can be a very valuable tool to inspire students to learn and a basis for formation of positive attitudes toward learning. A system of self-monitoring and evaluation is an important part of the student-centered, collaborative classroom. Some shared monitoring and self-evaluation strategies that we have found helpful are these:

1. Interviews and conferences with the instructor on a regular basis to discuss progress and problem areas using a monitoring sheet as a mediator.

2. Periodic self-monitoring or group monitoring using a prepared rating form.

3. A system of optional points that students may choose to earn toward their grades (where grading is required).

Some of these ideas may not be possible with beginning level students whose native language you do not speak, as the discussion and comprehension it requires to agree upon and carry out the procedures requires, at least, an intermediate level of proficiency.

We suggest that your discussion with the whole class on the first day of the term include the following clarifications about how the class will progress. For example:

1. Students will take responsibility for their successes or failures in this class.

2. Students will be advised and monitored on both language learning progress and on their participation in classroom activities.

3. Valuable learning opportunities will be lost if the assignments are not done.

4. Students will be recognized for all time and effort expended carrying out home and community-based assignments. Reporting of this extra-credit work will be accepted on an honor system.

5. Revision of paperwork will not be done by the teacher. The teacher will guide revision and it will be carried out by individual students or groups of students in conference.

Student Evaluation Strategy 1   **Progress Conferences**

Individual conferences with students let them know how you feel about their progress and participation; any academic problems they may be having are identified and discussed. Conferences can be called by either you or the student as often as is necessary to monitor progress and identify problems and solutions. We have found that using a Progress Form with a rating scale as a mediator can help to keep the conferences focused. Sometimes only the student fills in a Progress Form and talks about it with you. Other times you both will respond to a Progress Form and compare your perceptions. (See pages 49 and 50 for sample Progress Forms you may want to use as models in developing your own.)

Student Evaluation Strategy 2   **Monitoring Sheets**

Before you begin group tasks, tell students that at the end of the activity, they will be asked to rate themselves and their groups for active participation by turning in a Monitoring Sheet to the teacher. If students in a group actively participated in English during the entire task, they could, for example, receive a rating of 10. If they only sat and listened, they could rate themselves a 4 or 5. If they paid no attention and did not participate, they could rate themselves as 1. This evaluation strategy helps students be more aware of their own participation patterns as they are being carried out and provides feedback from group members. (See page 50 for sample Monitoring Sheet.)

Student Evaluation Strategy 3   **Extra Credit**

In addition to points earned for work turned in, for examinations, and for participation, students may earn extra credit for time they spend practicing their English outside the classroom. This system can be set up by the students themselves.

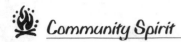

Start a list on the board of possible extra credit tasks. Have students brainstorm a list of other possibilities. What do they think will help their English improve? Decide together how many points each activity should earn. Create a check sheet and copy off a large stack of them for students to take and turn in weekly. Students seem to respond well to these self-determined point systems because they receive instant gratification for the tasks accomplished. They have a greater freedom to pursue the activity that interests them and to choose where, when, and how to carry out their practice. They are able to make up for poor performance in some areas by doing alternative activities.

If highly beneficial language learning activities, such as sustained silent reading and writing of compositions are given a higher point value than watching TV or filling in extra-credit worksheets, there is more incentive to attempt to carry out these tasks. Even in a program that doesn't assign grades, students still respond to the points they receive as acknowledgment of their efforts. (Sample extra-credit is on page 51.)

The greatest benefit of these types of student-determined point systems, we feel, is that both they and you are conscious of their daily personal efforts. Students are not graded only on exam scores, but on real, identifiable extra effort.

As students in our experience have been very honest on their self-ratings and extra-credit sheets, we believe that they should be trusted unless they have proven themselves to be untrustworthy. We may, however, remind ourselves and our students that teachers cannot be cheated. Students who cheat only cheat themselves out of valuable opportunities to make gain in their second-language. This is an attitude that may have to be continually fostered and reinforced with some groups. It may not be a shared value for all learners in your classroom.

Sample Progress Form #1

Student Self-Evaluation Meeting with the Teacher

NAME _____   Date _____

I come to school		sometimes	usually	every day
I am learning		a little bit		a lot
I have friends in class	one	two or three	several	many
I study at home	never	sometimes	often	always
English is		always difficult	sometimes difficult	easy
I like my class	not much	a little bit	most of the time	always

Sample Progress Form #2

Student Self-Evaluation Meeting with the Teacher

NAME _____   Date _____

I am	happy with my work	1 2 3 4 5	not happy with my work
My grammar	is improving	1 2 3 4 5	is not improving
My writing	is improving	1 2 3 4 5	is not improving
My speaking abiltity	is improving	1 2 3 4 5	is not improving
My reading ability	is improving	1 2 3 4 5	is not improving

The thing that was the hardest for me this week was _____

What I can do to learn English more quickly:

_____

_____

Sample Progress Form #3

Name_____   Date_____

1 = absolutely yes   8 = absolutely not

	Student self-rating	Teacher rating of student
I always do my best in this class.	1 2 3 4 5 6 7 8	1 2 3 4 5 6 7 8
I study outside of class.	1 2 3 4 5 6 7 8	1 2 3 4 5 6 7 8
I ask for help when I need it.	1 2 3 4 5 6 7 8	1 2 3 4 5 6 7 8
I have made an extra effort to reach goals that are important to me.	1 2 3 4 5 6 7 8	1 2 3 4 5 6 7 8
I am satisfied with my progress.	1 2 3 4 5 6 7 8	1 2 3 4 5 6 7 8
I am working well with my group.	1 2 3 4 5 6 7 8	1 2 3 4 5 6 7 8
I try to contact Americans outside of class	1 2 3 4 5 6 7 8	1 2 3 4 5 6 7 8
I am improving in my grammar.	1 2 3 4 5 6 7 8	1 2 3 4 5 6 7 8
I am improving in my speaking ability.	1 2 3 4 5 6 7 8	1 2 3 4 5 6 7 8
I am improving in my writing ability.	1 2 3 4 5 6 7 8	1 2 3 4 5 6 7 8
I am improving in my listening ability.	1 2 3 4 5 6 7 8	1 2 3 4 5 6 7 8
My reading is improving.	1 2 3 4 5 6 7 8	1 2 3 4 5 6 7 8

Group Participation Rating Sheet

Date:_____

1. I was an active participant. I talked, I listened and I assisted my group.

2. I talked and listened most of the time.

3. I talked and listened only a little today.

4. I only listened today.

5. I didn't participate today.

I rate *myself* today   _____

I rate my *group* today _____

EXTRA CREDIT FOR EXTRA EFFORT

Name_____

For the week of _____ to _____

I **watched TV in** [target language] **2 hours**	(1)
I **listened to talk radio in** [target language] **2 hours**	(1)
I **came to class every day this week**	(2)
I **asked questions during interviews**	(3)
I **attended listening lab 1 hour**	(4)
I **completed an extra homework assignment**	(4)
I **spoke only** [target language] **in class**	(5)
I **was an active participant in group work**	(5)
I **turned in a perfect paper**	(10)
I **had a conversation with a native speaker of** [target language]	(10)
I **read 10 extra pages in** [target language]	(10)
I **completed an oral or written book report**	(15)
I **wrote an extra full-page paper**	(15)
I **talked on the telephone for five minutes in** [target language]	(15)
I **called a business on the telephone for information**	(15)

What is the best way to assist students to form groups?

There are no definitive rules regarding the formation of groups. Procedures and choices vary from class to class and from one activity to the next. Groups may be formed according to teacher choice, by random selection, or by student choice. We can only experiment with a variety of methods to determine which work best with a particular group. Some important factors to consider when forming groups for collaborative, interactive tasks are student personalities, primary language background, gender, nationality, and age...and all the taboos and prejudices that may accompany these criteria!

Personality

Helpful and mature learners often work well with less mature learners in a teacher-student relationship. Competitive, impatient, more advanced students may pair up well. Two learners who have little self-confidence and low self-esteem as a rule do not make a good match. Nothing will get done.

Primary language

A class of learners from the same primary language background can be grouped well together across levels. It is also helpful to group like primary language students who are in the beginning levels so that they can ask for and give assistance to each other with content and process. In the higher levels, it is more desirable to mix the primary language backgrounds to help encourage students to speak as much English as possible.

Gender

In some cultures, women, in general, are kept segregated from men. Many women feel more comfortable with other women as partners. If paired with men, they may tend to hide their competence in the second language to avoid embarrassing the man. Romantic advances may occur when innocently pairing men with women. We need to recognize the possibility and be prepared to deal with the problems that may arise.

Nationality/Ethnicity

Some groups of learners have long standing fears or animosities toward each other. In adult ESL situations, for example, we cannot assume that two people from the same country or two people that speak the same primary language will be friendly and work well together. For example, two students from Laos may come from entirely different social strata and find nothing in common with each other. A Salvadoran and a Mexican, though both speak Spanish, may not be able to communicate with each other because of different social or political background. If you perceive you have age old prejudices boiling just beneath the surface smiles of your students, allow a little time to let your "sweet old peace-making self" work magic on them before pushing them into each other's laps.

Age

Young students usually learn quickly and may be impatient when paired with older students. However, as younger ones may be capable tutors, it is hard to make the decision not to put them in that position at times. As there may be some cultural taboos related to pairing of older and younger students, decide how important this factor is based on intuition and/or discussions with the students themselves.

Random grouping

Here are three of many methods for random grouping of students.

1. In a class of thirty students, select six group names. Write these group names on five slips of paper each. Students pull names from a box to find out which group they will be in.

2. Group students by months of their birth. Have them line up according to the month they were born beginning with January. When all are in line, the first four sit together, the second four sit together, etc.

3.. Count off around the class "1-2-3-4-5-6...1-2-3-4-5-6...1-2-3-4-5-6...etc." Then all the 1's sit together, all the 2's sit together, etc.

4. Fill a box with six colors of marbles. Students reach in, take a marble without looking, and sit down with matching color.

It is very possible that your students might want to work with existing, natural groups based on such factors as friendships, family members, age, ability, romance, interests, ethnicity, and that is also fine - at least some of the time. Often some of the most productive work can come from these self-selected groups. It really depends on the motivation and dedication of your students and is well worth a try.

It is not always necessary for groups to have the same number of students for every activity. If the task is a sharing of ideas, a brainstorm, a problem solving, then a slightly larger group (5-7) provides a wide variety of interesting input. Where the task focuses on meaningful, oral practice of material that has already been taught, smaller groups (2-3) give more time for each student to speak or take part. If the language work being carried out requires much teacher input, then the groups will have to be larger and fewer in number to make sure you have time to reach them all. Try to keep the group number consistent within any given activity. A group of three is more likely to finish a task sooner than a group of seven. If your groups are uneven, you will have to plan extra work for the small group to do while they are waiting for larger groups to complete their work.

In answer to the question "How long should students stay in the same group?" there is no one right answer. Sometimes it is appropriate for students to stay with the same group all quarter, all month, or all week. Other times the groups will be together for three minutes and then scramble to repeat the same short task with new partners. Observe your groups. Is work being accomplished? Are they being kind to each other? Glaring at each other? Is it just time to switch groups? Or is it time to give it a rest, open our workbooks to page 10 and fill in the blanks for a while?

We have attempted, so far, to offer you a strong rationale for implementing a more student-centered classroom, warned you of the nightmares you may be inviting, shared some remedies for chasing away those nightmares, and then given you some concrete strategies for getting students involved in the day to day work of keeping a classroom functioning, assisting each other, and monitoring their progress.

In Chapter Four we will discuss a variety of ways in which we may be better able to monitor our own progress as teachers committed to creating student-centered, collaborative language classrooms.

Chapter 4

KEEPING TABS

✦ *How can you, the teacher, monitor your own progress in moving toward a more student-centered, collaborative classroom?*

✦ *How can your students share in the evaluation of their classroom experience?*

```
TODAY, IN WHAT WAYS DID I SPECIFICALLY . . .

— focus on the learners rather than on myself?
— allow participation, rather than force it?
— respond to student input fairly?
— encourage divergent, critical, free thinking?
— stand back and wait?
— enlist student assistance in all aspects of the
  class experience?
— physically demonstrate confidence in myself? in
  them?
— leave my "authority" role behind and become a fel-
  low learner?
— give the students an opportunity to express their
  feelings?
— provide a variety of grouping strategies?
— arrange for students to tutor each other?
— allow students to choose the content or process of
  the lesson?
— organize real language practice, as opposed to
  mechanical?
— promote spontaneity/experimentation on the part of
  the learners?
— help students be aware of their achievement and
  successes?
— involve students in materials preparation?
```

Monitoring our own progress

The ideas presented in this text for building a student-centered, collaborative language classroom are just a beginning. They represent only the processes and strategies that we personally have experienced successfully with our learners. The content samples are based on what have been the particular needs, interests, and abilities of the students in our programs. Moreover, they have been limited by our own levels of creativity, and admittedly, by our own irascible and often incorrigible teacher-egos which still struggle to retain absolute control.

We still find it helpful to examine our own progress, our own movement toward letting go, by using a check-list of our own goals. Perhaps you will find this model useful in developing your own goal check-list.

Student evaluation of their classroom experience

Students are not always willing to express how they feel about their teacher or the class in which they are working...unless, of course they are paying a lot of money for the course; then they seem to be quite ready to voice their opinions! But we want to know what our students think. We want to know what they like and find helpful so that we can offer more of it. We need to know what they find unpleasant, boring, irrelevant, or a waste of time so that we can try a new implementation approach, offer a stronger rationale, or do whatever is necessary.

Anonymous rating sheets can be a non-threatening and effective way to survey student opinions, both complimentary and critical. Here is just one sample of an evaluative rating sheet. You may want to design one appropriate for your particular class and student population.

COURSE EVALUATION

1. I like this class.
       rarely   sometimes   usually   always

2. In this class I learn things that are important to me.
       rarely   sometimes   usually   always

3. The teacher organizes communication practice about real things.
       rarely   sometimes   usually   always

4. I feel like an equal member of this classroom.
       rarely   sometimes   usually   always

5. The teacher listens to the students with respect.
       rarely   sometimes   usually   always

6. The work we do in groups in this classroom is helpful for learning English.
       rarely   sometimes   usually   always

7. Our teacher lets us choose our topics and our learning activities democratically.
       rarely   sometimes   usually   always

8. The students in this classroom are encouraged to help each other and to ask each other for assistance.
       rarely   sometimes   usually   always

9. Whose classroom is this for the most part?
       the students' classroom   the teacher's classroom

10. Who talks the most in this classroom?
       the teacher   the students

The best thing about this class is _____

_____

The worst thing about this class is _____

_____

Something I'd like to see changed in this class is _____

_____

It would be easier to work in groups if _____

_____

OTHER COMMENTS _____

_____

_____

In these first four chapters we have taken you through all of the major ins, outs, ups and downs of developing a student-centered, collaborative classroom. The remainder of the text will offer you many practical, "I-can-use-it-tomorrow" type language practice strategies. We hope that these pages will provide a concrete model for versions and inventions of your own. You will find they are just a beginning.

Before heading off into the realm of language practice, we would like to make a few closing points. The main purpose of developing a student-centered, collaborative language classroom is to involve students more fully in their learning process. It is to help them learn not only the target language, but learn to interact more effectively in a work or social setting in the target language. It is also our objective to encourage them to develop more fully the skill of self-teaching which will be a life-long advantage.

In our student-centered classrooms over the years, we have observed learners who feel successful and confident, who are self-disciplined, who are independent thinkers and willing to listen to others and explore all possibilities. They converse because they have something to say, they listen because they truly want to hear, they read for information and enjoyment, and they write because they want to convey who they are and what they think. Their willingness to work together and learn from each other is evident even at the most basic beginning level, as illustrated by the following anecdote.

Azar, a fifty-year-old Iranian housewife is dictating numbers to her partner, Leong, who is 15 years old and from China. Both have been studying English less than a month.

"Sixteen," she says, from her side of the table. Leong writes "16," she writes "16," they compare papers to see if they have written the same number. So far, so good.

"Tier-tee-tree," she says. Leong hesitates. "Tier-tee-tree," she repeats slowly.

"Tier-tee-tree," she repeats somewhat loudly. "Tier-tee-tree!" I control my teacher impulse to jump in and bail them out.

Luisa, a Mexican woman at the next table sees the dilemma and comes to the rescue. "Leong...she say 'dudi-dree'...'dudi-dree,' Leong."

Leong shrugs his shoulders. Luisa scribbles "33" on her notebook cover and holds it up to him. Dawn breaks. He writes on his paper.

"Ah...fuh-tee-flea," he nods and smiles.

Their work continues.

These students are successfully on the road to collaborative language learning. It may be a slow journey made up of many false starts and sudden stops. They may find themselves going way back to retrieve bags of skills they left behind, or pulling out for rest-stops to unload preconceived notions collected on past learning trips. But throughout the entire experience they are coming to realize the advantages of conducting their own adventure. Their teacher-guide may provide the road maps, the enthusiastic voice of the seasoned traveler, a finger to point the way. But they choose the destination and the by-ways they will take to get there.

Chapter 5

INTERACTIVE STRATEGIES FOCUSING ON LANGUAGE ACQUISITION

✦ *How can you ensure that group tasks are productive?*

✦ *How can you organize group activities in your classroom?*

✦ *What are some generic strategies to begin with?*

How can we insure that group tasks are productive?

Before we begin talking about specific strategies and activities for the classroom, we would like you to consider again the skills that group members need in order for the group to be successful, to run smoothly and to be a positive experience for all the members involved. In Chapter Two (page 28), we introduced some necessary skills that learners must have to work effectively in groups. As we all know, students do not usually come to our classrooms with these skills perfectly formed. However, we can assist our students in building these skills in our classrooms over time. One way we as teachers help our students with these skills is to go through a checklist periodically and check off the skills our students are having difficulty in developing. Then, we can focus our activities on helping students use these skills. This is not an exhaustive list by any means; it's just a beginning. Add your own ideas.

CHECKLIST ONE
What skills do our students have for working in groups?

Make a (✔) beside the skills that your students need to develop.

1. ____ Can students form groups quickly and without making noise that will disturb others?

2. ____ Can students stay in the groups they are assigned to? Do they refrain from moving to other groups and disturbing other students?

3. ____ Do students participate in their groups using quiet voices?

4. ____ Do students set-up a turn-taking process to determine roles for the members in the group?

5. ____ Can students perform various roles in the group, acting as note takers, monitors, readers, and reporters?

6. ____ Do students in the group use each other's names?

7. ____ Do students refrain from using "put downs" or argumentative behavior in the group?

8. ____ Do group members pay attention to and listen to the speaker?

9. ____ Do group members know how to clarify assignments with the teacher or group?

10. ____ Do group members know how to watch for time limits and pace their work accordingly?

11. ____ Are group members learning how to express support and find out what other members are thinking?

12. ____ Do group members know how to ask for clarification and elaborate on others' ideas or opinions?

13. ____ Can the group members summarize another's comments and offer explanations for why things are happening?

14. ____ Do group members know how to correct each other in a polite and supportive way when someone in the group gives incorrect information?

15. ____ Are group members learning how to criticize ideas without criticizing people?

16. ____ Do group members know how to ask for justification for answers and conclusions?

Developing group tasks

All of us want to implement successful language tasks in our classrooms. We have found that working with the factors below has helped us in developing group tasks. If you find the list useful, we hope you will add any other ideas that come to mind. We use this list in the same way we use the list of necessary skills for group work. As we develop language tasks, we review the list and place a check by those that need some work.

CHECKLIST TWO
Factors to consider in designing activities

Use this checklist to make sure you have "covered all bases" before implementing any group task.

_____ 1. Is the activity highly structured physically, spatially, and temporally? Students want to know: Who will they work with? Who will go first? Second? What will they use? How much time do they have as a group or individually? What is the process?

_____ 2. Do students know the rationale for an activity? Do students know why they are doing this activity? Do they know how it will help them improve their language abilities?

_____ 3. How will this activity help them as language learners? Students need to know: How will group work help them? What opportunities will they have for interaction? Will they be able to share information? Will they learn how to compromise, negotiate, take turns as leaders, create new things, practice the democratic process and feel success with the group?

_____ 4. What is expected of them by the teacher? Do group members know what you expect them to have, show you, turn in, know, or tell others when they have finished the activity?

_____ 5. How will the learning activity affect motivation? Will the students be motivated to participate in the activity? Is the activity fun? Interesting? Valuable?

_____ 6. Does the activity accommodate various group speeds? When some groups complete the activity early, what do they do?

_____ 7. How long will the activity take? How much time will be spent listening? How much time will be spent speaking? Have you given them a task much longer than their attention span?

_____ 8. How will the students feel when the activity has been completed? Is there something built into the activity that will guarantee some sort of satisfaction when the activity has been completed? How can you show them success?

_____ 9. How do you encourage students to use the target language and discourage use of the native language in small group work? What "back-up" devices can you utilize to remind students to use the target language?

_____10. Does the structure of the activity give students time to process the new information before they are asked to respond? Is reflection time built into the activity?

_____11. Do the topics chosen for the activities give students a chance to talk about what they know? Do they have an opportunity to show you and the other members in the group what they know?

What are some generic language learning strategies?

Through our language teaching experiences in the past twenty years, we have identified many different generic strategies that are ideal for pair or small group practice. We will present seven strategies which vary in complexity of process. Some of the strategies are easy procedures to manage, such as card and picture manipulation tasks. There are also more complex or sophisticated processes such as jigsaw and problem solving activities.

Within each of these seven generic strategies, it is possible to vary the difficulty of the content or the language items practiced. This makes it possible to use each strategy many times at all levels of instruction without resulting in boredom on the part of the students. For example, one strategy is "sorting and classifying." It is a relatively simple process. It may entail sorting pictures or single words or sentences. It may be something as linguistically easy as categorizing a mixed stack of vocabulary cards according to months, food, and professions under the correct heading. Advanced students might be given a list of adverbs, adjectives, and verbs to sort and classify, using them later in sentences and defending their decisions. By careful selection of strategies according to both process and content, students will experience step-by-step independent interaction techniques. They can feel success from the first moment.

In this chapter, we want to outline each strategy and offer you several samples of content that you might consider. The content you use will be entirely dependent upon the age, interests, goals, and language needs of your particular students. The content in this chapter is very general. Once you become familiar with the strategies and how they work, you will want to choose content that is more specific to your own classroom. You can reinforce, review, and practice a wide variety of content within these strategies. We know that the ideas we present here for your consideration are only a beginning. We hope you will use them as a springboard for your own creative efforts.

Language learning strategies

MATCHING or CONCENTRATION

General process

The instructor prepares and duplicates* two different worksheets with related content (words, pictures, sentences). Students work in pairs. Student A gets worksheet A; student B, worksheet B. First, individual students must cut or carefully tear their worksheets into individual "cards." (Examples to follow.)

There are two different ways that matching activities can be conducted. Students may stay seated and be asked to work with a partner. Many teachers also like to conduct activities with students moving around. For a *matching* activity with students seated at their desks, students place their cards face up on the desk in front of them. Student A selects one of the cards for student B to match. Then Student B takes a B card for student A to match. The turn taking process continues until all the cards have been matched. Then, students read the matches aloud to each other. Helping between groups is encouraged if neither partner can determine the correct match. For a matching activity with students milling around, use a set of matched A and B cards for the whole group. Give one card to each student. Ask them to mill around until they find their partner– the person who matches their card.

For a *concentration* activity, students put all the cards together, mixing them well. These are placed face *down* on the table or desk in an orderly fashion so that each card is visible with the back side up. Student A selects a card at random, turns it over, and names it. Then, s/he turns over another random card to see if the two cards match. If they do not, then both cards are turned back over in their place. If they do match, Student A keeps the cards. Then Student B tries to make a match by turning over two cards at random. Students must concentrate on remembering where the different cards are located so they can make a match. The process continues until all cards are matched and won.

---

*In this book when we say *duplicate,* we mean one of the following:
  1. Prepare a spirit master or photocopy master from original material,
  2. trace, retype or rewrite material from your classroom set of textbooks onto a spirit master or photocopy master,
  3. photocopy material from your classroom set of textbooks, or
  4. photocopy from any published work for which permission has been given to reproduce according to the *fair use for education* practice as established by the US. Copyright laws.

Sometimes it may be a good idea to give the cards to the students to take home for a review. It is also very handy to collect these cards, paper-clip them together in sets, and store them in small coin envelopes so they can be used over and over again.

Samples of content

The following pages will show you some *samples* of content which may be used for different level students. These are general, generic topics. We know that you will think of many different topics to use in matching and concentration. The possibilities are limitless!

A		B	
B	D	s	g
F	C	j	b
J	G	d	i
H	l	r	f
Q	R	q	l
L	S	h	c

**Sample 1
MATCHING**

Upper and Lower Case

**Sample 2
MATCHING**

**Numbers and
Symbols**

A		B	
7	2	six	one
6	9	twelve	three
1	3	eight	seven
8	10	two	nine
4	11	ten	five
12	5	four	eleven

**Sample 3
MATCHING**

**Pictures
and Words:
Clothing**

A.		B.	
(sock)	(shoe)	hat	scarf
(hat)	(shorts)	pants	shoe
(t-shirt)	(jacket)	glasses	sweater
(glasses)	(scarf)	blouse	sock
(skirt)	(bikini)	jacket	T-shirt
(blouse)	(sweater)	bikini	skirt

A. **B.**

[money]	[face]	Do you like American music?	Do you write letters to your friends?
[cat]	[California]	Do you like to eat fish?	Do you have a car?
[apple]	[envelope/letter]	Do you need more money?	Do you ride the bus to school?
[bus]	[milk carton and glass]	Do you live in California?	Do you want an apple?
[radio with music notes]	[fish]	Do you have a cat?	Do you drink milk?

**Sample 4
MATCHING**

Pictures and Sentences: Basic questions, Like, Have, Want

A B

When did he begin work?	Where did she eat lunch?	He started at 8:00 am.	In the coffee shop.
How did he go to work?	Why did he work so much?	He worked at a garage.	Susan did.
Who rode to work with her?	When did she go to work?	Because he needed money.	He drove his old car.
Where did he work last year?	How many days did he work?	He worked alone.	He liked to repair cars.
What did he like about his work?	In which bank does she work?	No, she didn't.	She went early in the morning.
Did she like her work?	Who did he work with?	She works at Pacific Bank.	Six days a week.

**Sample 5
MATCHING**

Questions and Answers: WH-questions

Sample 6
MATCHING
Comments and Responses

A.	B.
Nice to meet you.	Nothing much.
See you later.	Yes, you're welcome.
Oh, no!	That's okay.
May I open the door?	Pretty well, thanks.
Hurry up!	Go ahead.
What's going on?	Good to meet you, too.
Thanks!	So long.
How's it going?	What happened?
Wait a minute!	I can't. I am late!
How are you?	I'm coming! Don't rush me.
I'm sorry.	No, thank you
May I help you?	Very well!

Sample 7
MATCHING
Words and Definitions

A	B
to chase	many steps
ball point	in the middle
pull over	gold and jewels
stairs	to run after
between	a tool for digging
whale	a kind of pen
treasure	to watch in secret
shovel	a kind of sweater
to call on	garbage
to spy	a large sea animal
puppy	a baby dog
rubbish	to ask for help

comma	!
period	« »
question mark	'
exclamation	.
parentheses	:
quotation marks	*
apostrophe	?
colon	,
semi-colon	( )
dash	;
asterisk	/
slash	—

**Sample 8
MATCHING**

**Punctuation
Marks**

A	B
tall	thin
rich	new
brunette	difficult
chubby	short
old	late
shy	poor
older	happy
early	blonde
quickly	out-going
single	younger
easy	married
sad	slowly

**Sample 9
MATCHING**

Antonyms

**Sample 10
MATCHING**

**Signs and
Meanings**

		barbershop	fires permitted
		women's restroom	post office
		bar night club	no parking
		prescriptions, drug store	men's restroom
		school crossing	picnic grounds
		medical aid	Poison do not eat or drink

SEQUENCING

General process

Sequencing activities give students the opportunity to work in pairs or small groups with a task that focuses on arranging small cards or paper strips in their proper or logical order. Materials are prepared by either the teacher or the students.

We begin the activity by setting a time limit, usually 10 to 15 minutes. Each pair or group of students is given one set of cards or paper strips from the main "bank" and asked to put them in a certain order that makes some lexical, grammatical or semantic sense. All students will be working simultaneously; some will work faster than others. When students complete their sequence in a way they all agree is correct, they call the instructor over to check their work. If it is not correct, the teacher may help by pointing out where the error lies or simply encourage them to try again, with no hints. Intergroup help is also encouraged. When students finish their sequence correctly, they mix up the cards or strips, clip them back together, return the set to the "bank" and take another set to work on. The process continues until time is up; some students will get through ten different sequences, while others may only solve two or three.

The following sample content for sequencing ranges from the most simple to the most complex. These are only examples. The best content is that which complements your class text and your students needs and interests.

If you would like your students to become involved in the materials development for these activities, remind them to write carefully and clearly, using manuscript letters so that all students are able to read them easily. Also, with content that focuses on vocabulary or grammar patterns, you may find it helpful to have students find and select the words and sentences in their textbook (in a unit or units named by the instructor) to avoid misspellings and incorrect grammar! Of course, you will want to check all final products carefully before adding them to the materials bank.

Sample 1
SEQUENCING

Word Forming

Students work in pairs or small groups forming words from prepared letter sets which have been clipped together and stored in a "bank." These letter sets can be prepared by the instructor in about a half hour, using 2" X 3" cards, the vocabulary list from previously studied units in the text, and markers. Or, they may be prepared by the students in class in less than 10 minutes, by letting them look in the vocabulary lists, giving them a stack of blank cards and markers and paper clips and reminding them to be scrupulously careful in their writing and spelling! Check their words as they offer them to you for the materials "bank" to be sure they are correct.

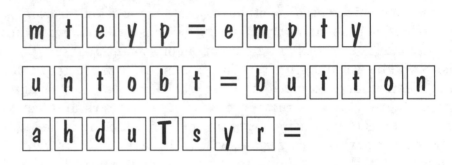

Sample 2
SEQUENCING

Jumbled
Sentences

This is essentially the same exercise as above and may be prepared in the same way as described above. The only difference is that students will be working with word cards to form correct sentences. Remember, this is a time limit activity, with some students having time to accomplish more sets than others. This is perfectly acceptable. All students are busily working collaboratively, at their own speed while assisting each other.

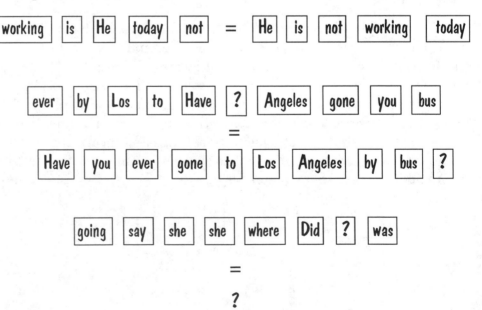

Directions: the following paragraphs are not presented in the correct order. Read the paragraphs with your partner. Then decide which paragraph should come first, second, etc. Mark the order by writing a number in the blank space at the beginning of the paragraph. Prepare to explain to the entire class why you made the decisions you did.

Paragraph # _____
It is important to prepare the soil properly. You need to till the soil in the early spring and give it a boost of fertilizer. Many people buy a special machine to till and work the soil, but you can also work a little harder and turn the soil with a shovel. This works well if your garden is not too large. After you have finished turning the soil, add the fertilizer. The best fertilizer is the natural kind. You can buy manure in large bags and dump it on the garden. Then, mix the soil and the manure together. Then, rake the soil in order to smooth it out and water it well. Let it sit for several days.

Paragraph # _____
More and more people in the United States are paying attention to eating healthy food. It is not surprising, then, that in the past few years there has been an increase in home gardening. People are interested in growing food at home. If you have never had your own garden, you may be a little bit apprehensive. Can I really do it? Can I grow fruits and vegetables for my family and do it the first time? The answer to these questions is, "yes." It is easy to grow your own produce, cheaper, and also healthier to have freshly grown fruits and vegetables that have escaped many of the chemicals used on commercial farms. Follow these five simple steps.

Paragraph # _____
The next step is determining where to plant the different items in your garden. Take a piece of paper and sketch it out. Remember to plant corn at the back of the garden and all in one place. Allow about 6-9 inches between rows. Corn and potatoes will take more space because they will have to be hilled.

Paragraph # _____
After you have planted all of your seeds, you must next think about water. If you plant your garden in the early spring, you will not have much trouble keeping it wet. The sun is not too hot and the soil will stay damp longer. If you plant your garden later, you will have to water it several times a day. You must use the gentle spray on your lawn sprayer. Keep the garden watered in this way until all of the rows of vegetables are up and the rows are clearly visible. Once they are visible, you can make small furrows or ditches and water the new plants from the roots.

Paragraph # _____
The last step is probably the most difficult. You must wait! Think about all the wonderful food that will soon grace your dinner table. And while you are waiting, don't forget about the water. A good garden digests plenty of water. Oh yes, did we mention the weeds? You will need to weed every few days. A healthy patch of weeds has been known to spoil an otherwise productive garden. Good luck!

Paragraph # _____
Once you have decided where to plant your vegetables, it is time to plant. First, you make shallow ditches in the soil. You can do this with the side of the hoe. Then, you need to run water down these small ditches. Next, scatter the seeds according to the directions given on the seed packet. Once you have scattered the seeds, cover them very carefully with a small amount of dirt and tamp the covered seeds down carefully with the side of the hoe.

Follow-up questions
How did you decide on the correct order? What specific words or phrases did you use to help you decide? Write the words or phrases here.

Paragraph #1 _____

_____

Paragraph #2 _____

_____

Paragraph #3 _____

_____

Paragraph #4 _____

_____

Paragraph #5 _____

_____

Compare your answers with another group. Did you have the same answers?

**Sample 4
SEQUENCING**

**Jumbled
Sentences**

This activity is the same as the previous task, except that it is a disarranged dialog rather than a story passage, and students work in pairs only. The dialog may be duplicated from one in the textbook your students are using, a slight variation of one they have practiced, or an entirely original one. Again, each pair of students gets one copy of the same dialog. One partner separates the lines. Students work together to arrange them in a sensible order. When this is accomplished, the dialog can be used in a usual manner - reading together, reciting, memorizing, rewriting, isolating new vocabulary and patterns, etc.

"That's a lot of food."
- - - - - - - - - - - - - - - - - -
"Right here!"
- - - - - - - - - - - - - - - - - -
"Where's the coffee?"
- - - - - - - - - - - - - - - - - -
"Hi, Paul! What are you doing here?"
- - - - - - - - - - - - - - - - - -
"It's next to the fish."
- - - - - - - - - - - - - - - - - -
"What are you buying?"
- - - - - - - - - - - - - - - - - -
"And, where's the fish?"
- - - - - - - - - - - - - - - - - -
"They are over there, next to the meat."
- - - - - - - - - - - - - - - - - -
"I'm buying food for my family."
- - - - - - - - - - - - - - - - - -
"Where's the meat?"
- - - - - - - - - - - - - - - - - -
"A lot. Here's the list."
- - - - - - - - - - - - - - - - - -
"It's next to the tea."
- - - - - - - - - - - - - - - - - -
"Where are the apples?"

You can make your own "confounded cartoons" very easily. Duplicate a 6 to 8 picture cartoon strip from the Sunday paper. Cut the pictures apart and paste them back together in a scrambled order on a sheet of paper. Make several copies of this sheet. Put the students in pairs or threes (depending on how many characters are interacting in the cartoon) and give each group one sheet of cartoon squares. Students will cut or carefully tear apart the pictures. Then, they will work together to decide on an order. (We have found that "Blondie," "Hi and Lois," and "Cathy" make excellent choices. They usually deal with day to day activities that are universal in their appeal.) When the task is complete, have each student take the part of one character. They should practice in their groups and then present their "comedy" to the entire class. Follow-up with a class discussion about why it is funny.

**Sample 5
SEQUENCING**

**Confounded
Cartoons**

Blondie By Young & Drake

Reprinted with special permission of King Features Syndicate.

**Sample 6
SEQUENCING
Alphabet Soup**

On an 8 X 10 sheet (or spirit master) write a number of words within a grid, perhaps ten words for beginners, up to 25 for more advanced students. Make several copies. Give each pair or group of students one sheet. One student will separate the words on the lines to make cards. The group works together to arrange the words in alphabetical order on the table. When all groups have completed the task, work with the words orally or in writing. We suggest using only words that have been previously studied for beginning students, and perhaps words in "categories," e.g. all verbs, all nouns, all household items, all occupations. Following are two sample content ideas for beginning level students.

Example Alphabet Soup: Food

eggs	ice cream
jam	apples
bananas	lemons
nuts	fish
grapes	hot dogs
mayonnaise	cookies
doughnuts	oranges

Example Alphabet Soup: Computers

floppy disk	hard drive
software	word processing
save	print
delete	lab assistant
text	memory
keystroke	screen
monitor	keyboard
mouse	electronic mail

Write a simple "recipe" in a scrambled fashion in a grid. Divide students into pairs or groups. Give one copy of the grid to each pair or small group. Each group will cut the recipe into strips. They will work together to try to arrange the recipe in logical order. After you have presented this type of content several times in your class, suggest that the students write their own recipes for homework and bring them to be used in class. (Give them blank grids to work with and remind them of the importance of clear, clean, manuscript writing.) You will want to check recipes for spelling, grammar, etc. before you make the final copy.

Sample 7
SEQUENCING

What's Cooking?

**Sample 8
SEQUENCING**

**Which Comes
First?**

Write a series of directions for performing a well-known task. Write each step on a separate line. Give one step to each student. Have them memorize what is on their papers. Collect the papers. Have them interact with each other and put the task back together again in the correct order. After having worked with this sort of content, your students will be able to write their own instructions. They will write about tasks that are of interest to their particular group. Save their work in small envelopes for future use.

Making a phone call

You remember that you have to make a phone call to a friend and don't know her number.	Take the phone book from the desk drawer.
Pick up the receiver and dial your friend's number.	Put the phone book away.
Dial your friend's number again. This time the phone is ringing.	Your friend answers the phone on the third ring. She is happy to hear from you.
Look up the friend's telephone number in the phone book. Write the number on a piece of paper.	Wait for the phone to ring. Too bad! You get the busy signal.
Wait 5 minutes and call back again.	

Going to the Laundry

Put the clothes in the washing machine.	Put the clothes in the dryer.
Put the quarters in the dryer	Drink a soda while you are waiting for the clothes to wash.
Separate the clothes into three piles: white, colored and very dirty.	Take the clothes out of the dryer.
Close the washing machine.	Read a magazine while you are waiting for the clothes to dry.
Add soap.	Take the clothes out of the washer.
Wait until the machine fills with water.	Fold the clothes.
Put the quarters in the washing machine.	Carry your basket into the laundry.

CLASSIFYING AND SORTING

General procedure

In these activities students will be asked to work together to find relationships among general items by classifying and sorting. Students will be divided into pairs or small groups. There will be one worksheet for each pair or group. Only one group member will write. The idea of intergroup sharing and collaboration will be introduced.

Sample 1
CLASSIFYING AND SORTING

Parts of Speech Treasure Hunt

```
Directions: Review the eight parts of speech with
your teacher and classmates (noun, verb, adverb,
adjective, preposition, pronoun, interjection,
conjunction). Be certain you understand what each
part of speech represents. Then, work with a
partner. Decide which one of you will write. Read
the following paragraph. Then, put each word in
the paragraph in the appropriate word category
depending on how it is used in the paragraph.
Write the words in the chart where you think they
belong. Check your answers with your classmates
and with the teacher.

TREASURE HUNTER'S PARAGRAPH
My family and I moved to Ephraim, Utah. Alas! It
was not the same as New York City! We do many
things here that we did not do in the city. We
hike and swim in the summer and ski and skate in
the winter. If you want an active life, you will
like Utah.

Parts of Speech Treasure Hunt

    Nouns           Verbs           Pronouns




    Adverbs         Adjectives      Prepositions




    Conjunctions                    Interjections


```

PARTS OF SPEECH TREASURE HUNT ANSWER KEY

Nouns
family, Ephraim, Utah, New York City, things, city, summer, winter, life

Verbs
moved, was, do, did, hike, swim, ski, want, will, like, skate

Pronouns
I, it, we, that, you

Adverbs
as, here

Adjectives
my, not, many, a, the, an, active, same

Prepositions
to, in

Conjunctions
and, if

Interjections
Alas

Sample 2
CLASSIFYING AND SORTING

Parts of Speech Categories

Directions: Look at the words below. Put them in the proper category. If you think the words belong in more than one category, give example sentences that clearly show the word being used in each category.

ADVERB	VERB	NOUN	ADJECTIVE

Collective	Interest	Creation	Bore
Collection	Interesting	Creative	Boredom
Collectable	Interested	Creatively	Boring
Collected	Interestingly	Create	Bored
Collectively	Interestedly	Created	Boringly

Sample 3
CLASSIFYING AND SORTING

Things That Fly; Things That Fold

Directions: Choose five categories from the list below. Make a list of eight things that fit in each category. Then, make a master list with the words in scrambled order. Give your master list to another group. Their task will be to think of five categories that the words will fit into and put them into these categories. Compare lists. Did you have the same categories? Different categories?

Choose five categories from the list below.

Animals
Things in a classroom
World holidays
Things you can peel
Things that fold
Things you can hang up
Things you can plug in
Things that fly
Flowers
Sweet things
Things you can drink
Things you use for cleaning
Things found in a bedroom
Things found in a kitchen

Directions: Put the words below in FOUR groups.

DESK	DRESS	TABLE	BOOK	ICE CREAM	BUS
APPLE	PENCIL	PEACH	PEN	NOTEBOOK	TRAIN
SHOES	SOCKS	POTATOES	RULER	BLACKBOARD	BANANAS
SHIRT	SUIT	ERASER	CAR	MOTORCYCLE	PANTS
FRENCH FRIES	PIE	CANDY	SHIP	AIRPLANE	INK
GARBAGE CAN	PAPER	TAPE	SLIP	TIE	

GROUP #1 _____

GROUP #2 _____

GROUP #3 _____

GROUP #4 _____

Sample 4
CLASSIFYING AND SORTING
Noun Categories

Cut, sort, read aloud, copy.		
yellow	jacket	fireman
doctor	three	sweater
shorts	red	seven
nine	fourteen	secretary
blue	mechanic	eight
fifteen	jeans	green
blouse	dishwasher	fifty
teacher	orange	housewife

Sample 5
CLASSIFYING AND SORTING
Sort The Words

CHARTS AND GRIDS

General procedure and information

A grid is a series of boxes (called "cells") formed by overlapping horizontal rows and vertical columns. Such grids can be manipulated in many different ways as the basis of language teaching activities. You can also alter the size of the grid to make the activities easier or more difficult depending on the proficiency of the learners.

Sample 1
CHARTS AND GRIDS
WH Questions

The students listen as the teacher dictates a series of WH questions about the various class members. The students copy the questions on their blank grids. The students must then circulate with their grids and ask each other the questions. When they ask a question and get a response, they get the person's signature. Then, they must move on to another person. You can only sign each grid once! The activity continues until all the students have filled all the cells with signatures (the longer version) or until one students gets five signatures in a row for a "bingo" (the shorter version).

Sample 2
CHARTS AND GRIDS
Drawing Grids

The teacher distributes two blank grids with 6 large cells to each student. On one grid, the students draw from one to five objects in each cell. Then, each student is given a blank grid and in pairs the students describe their own grid pictures to their partners to draw. When the drawings and the descriptions are complete, the students compare the original with the replica.

Pairs of students practice with a grid including students' names and pictures that are hand drawn or cut from magazines. (Charts are created by the teacher or by the students themselves.) They may practice forming questions and answers or simply form sentences. Practice may be only oral or may include having students write questions and answers for each other.

"What did Ali buy at Sears?"   "He bought a hammer."
"How much did it cost?"   "It cost $12.00."
"Sitha bought a jacket at Mervyn's department store for $29.00."

Another variation of this grid is to use days of the week at the top. The pictures in the cells depict activities.

	MONDAY	THURSDAY	SATURDAY
SAM	LAUNDRY	CAR	PARK
LUISA	IRONING	MARKET	DANCE
MEI / LIN	STUDYING	SKATING	T.V.

"What is Sam going to do on Thursday?"   "He's going to fix his car."
"Are Mei and Lin going to watch TV on Monday?"
"No, they are going to study English."

**Sample 4
CHARTS AND
GRIDS**

**Interaction
Matrices**

General procedure

Ahead of time, give each student four pieces of 9 X 12 construction paper in four different colors and one marking pen. Taking about five minutes of class time, have them prepare matrices that you will be able to use over and over again in your class. (This saves you at least two hours of homework!)

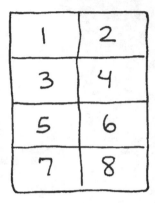 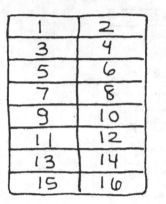 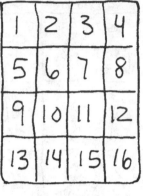 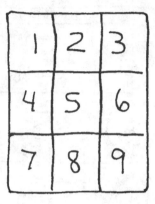

Any colors will do, but be sure that all 8-square matrices are one color, all 12-square matrices are another color, etc. (This is simply for ease of collection, storing, and handing out.)

For an interaction matrix exercise, students work in pairs. All students are given an identical worksheet which they will cut up into "cards." All pairs have identical matrices, this stack of cards and a partner. Between the partners stands a manila file folder on end so that they are unable to see each others' matrices.

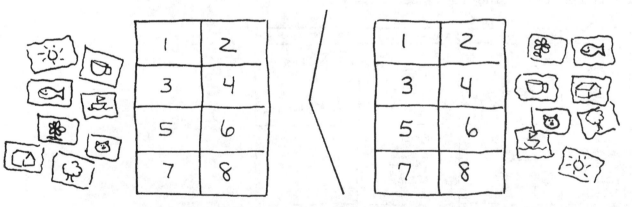

To begin the activity, Student A selects at random one of her cards and places it on her matrix square number one. She names (or describes or reads) the card for her partner and instructs him to place it on number one. Student B finds the card in his set and places it on his own matrix and the process continues.

> *"Number 2 - It is a lamp."*
> *"Number 3 - They are sofas."*
> *"Number 4 - It is a refrigerator."*

When all cards are in place on the matrices, the barrier is removed. Students compare the order of their cards to see if they are identical. Then, they gather up the cards, shuffle them, switch roles, and go through the process one more time.

The content may focus on vocabulary, sentences, grammar, or phonics and pronunciation. It may be in the form of pictures only, words only, a combination of pictures and words, or sentences. If pictures are desired, they may be found and duplicated from magazines, your classroom set of texts, newspapers, or drawn free hand.* When the activity is over, you may want students to take the cards home for practice, or you may decide to clip the sets together and keep them in your materials bank for use over and over. (This will save you time, money, energy and materials for next time.)

If you are using pictures to cue the oral language, you must first give a clear model of what you expect from the students. For example, if you were using pictures of places around town, depending on the level of your group and the focus of the activity, you could model any one of the following:

A. "Number 1 - Bank"
   "Number 2 - Market"
   "Number 3 - Drugstore"

B. "Number 1 - "Is he at the bank?"
   "Number 2 - "Is he at the market?"
   "Number 3 - "Is he at the drugstore?"

C. "Number 1 - "He didn't go to the bank. He went to the park."
   "Number 2 - "He didn't go to the museum. He went to the market."
   "Number 3 - "He didn't go to the drugstore. He went to the hospital."

D. "Number 1 - "Where has he gone? He's gone to the bank."
   "Number 2 - "Where has he gone? He's gone to the market."
   "Number 3 - "Where has he gone? He's gone to the drug store."

The following pages give several examples of matrix content sheets illustrating the use of pictures, words, and sentences, and showing how the focus may be changed from pronunciation to grammar, from vocabulary to stories. Use them as a guide, and then rely on your own imagination. The content sheets you make can be used time and time again, most can be made very quickly. The students never seem to get bored with this type of strategy because each time the content, the focus, and the partner change! We have received more positive comments, both from students and other teachers alike, on this strategy than on any other techniques we have taught or used.

---

*See bibliography for three excellent sources of pictures for interaction matrices:
The Basic Vocabulary Builder, Verbs, Verbs, Verbs, and *Sounds Easy!*

**Example
Interaction
Matrix**

Story Sequence

ALONE / SMALL HOUSE	MEXICO	FACTORY
old FORD	HAMBURGERS EAT EAT	cook
ADULT SCHOOL	friends	coffee
WORKS	SATURDAY NIGHT	USA / MEXICO

Script

Billy lives alone in a small house.

His family is in Mexico.

He works everyday in a factory.

He drives an old Ford to work.

After work, he usually eats in a cheap restaurant.

He doesn't like to cook.

Sometimes he goes to school in the evening.

He sees his friends there.

He drinks coffee with his friends.

On Saturday, Billy works on his old car.

He listens to music with his friends on Saturday night.

Usually, he calls his mother on Sunday, but it is very expensive.

**Example
Interaction
Matrix**

Vocabulary

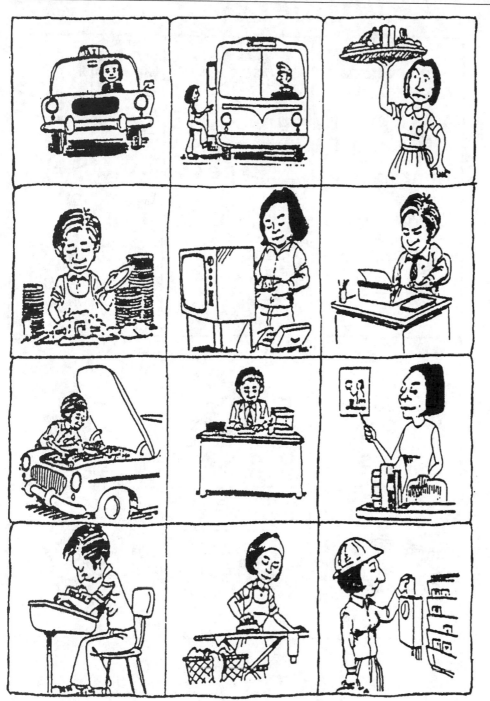

Script

taxi driver	mechanic
bus driver	businessman
waitress	teacher
dishwasher	student
repairman	housewife
secretary	factory worker

Example Interaction Matrix

Everyday Activities

Script

It's 7:00 in the morning.
Go back to sleep.
It's 7:45. Wake up!
Get out of bed.
Take a bath
Put on your clothes.

Tie your shoes.
Eat your breakfast.
Brush your teeth.
Comb your hair.
Get on the bus.
Go to school.

**Example
Interaction
Matrix**

Phonics

**Sample 5
CHARTS
AND GRIDS**

**Maps and
Directions**

Students should sit back-to-back or place a file folder between them. Each student gets a copy of a blank map. Each student follows the directions at the top of the map. Then, Student A will give directions to Student B for completing her map in the same way. Student B will do the same. The activity is finished when both maps look the same. Talk about any changes you need to make. Students should check their work by comparing maps.

Student A Map
1) Name all streets running east and west. 2) Draw a library, movie house, drugstore and your house.

Student B Map
1) Name all streets running north and south. 2) Draw a bank, grocery store, swimming pool, school, and your house.

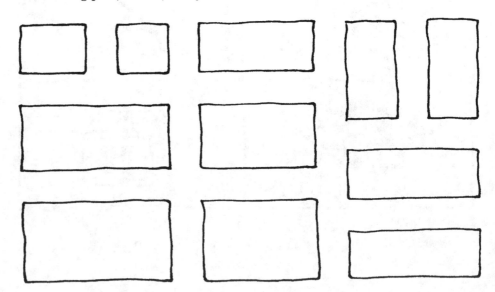

Students complete the blanks in their grid by getting information from their partner. Sometimes it will be necessary to answer a question. Other times missing information will need to be supplied. For example, student A asks, "What's in square #2?" and student B will either give a question or provide missing information. The listening student will write the answer of the missing information, not the speaking student's exact words.

**Sample 6
CHARTS
AND GRIDS**

Grammar Grid

Form A

1. What's the past tense of to go? to study? to quit?	2.	3. what's the past tense of to sit? to eat? to put?
4. What's the past tense of to sleep? to eat? to think?	5.	6. What are the first person pronouns?
7.	8. What goes in the blank? He was _____ even after 10 hours of sleep.	9.
10.	11. Name one relative pronoun.	12.

Form B

1.	2. Choose: Bill (take/takes)_____ everything too seriously.	3.
4.	5. Choose: (Does/Do)_____ you want a coke?	6.
7. Choose: Bill was (help/helping) _____ his father.	8.	9. Name one coordinating conjunction.
10. What is the second person pronoun?	11.	12. Name one subordinating conjunction.

**Sample 7
CHARTS
AND GRIDS**

**What Are
They Saying?**

Students work with a partner. Partner A takes the picture page entitled "What are they saying?" (next page), and a piece of scratch paper. He numbers his scratch paper from 1 to 9. Partner B reads the statements in the box below. Partner A decides which person on the picture page is making that statement and marks the letter on the piece of scratch paper.

1. D	4.	7.
2. C	5.	8.
3. H	6.	9.

When notations for all nine pictures are complete, students switch roles and do the task again. Then they compare their notations. (There are, of course, no "correct" answers.) As a follow up, have partners create all new statements for each picture and share some of them with the whole class.

```
Statements for the What are they saying? Grid.

1. Strike three?? Are you crazy?

2. I'm not worried. It'll grow back again in a
   few weeks.

3. Wow!  Thanks for doing the dishes!

4. Sure! I'd love to go with you to the movies.

5. I have to do my homework before I go to the
   dance?

6. Maybe I should ask your girlfriend to the dance.

7. I just can't stay awake!

8. He makes me so angry!

9. My stomach hurts and I have a headache.

Discuss the answers your partner has chosen.
```

Possible answers:

Statement 1 - picture G

Statement 2 - picture C

Statement 3 - picture C, E or I

Statement 4 - picture C, E or I

Statement 5 - picture A, B or D

Statement 6 - picture C, E or F

Statement 7 - picture A or H

Statement 8 - picture D or G

Statement 9 - picture A or B

What Are They Saying?

**Sample 8
CHARTS
AND GRIDS**

**Calendar
Grid**

Form A

Directions: Work with a partner. Each partner has a calendar and a list of events. You are partner A. Write the following six events somewhere on your calendar. Tell your partner where to write these events on his calendar. Don't look at each other's calendars! Partner B will tell you six more events to add to your calendar. Please listen and write them in. When you are finished, look at your calendars together and answer the questions. Write your answers.

Calendar Events for Partner A

Mary's birthday
Dinner with the Wilsons (7:00 pm)
Appointment with the dentist (1:00 pm)
Haircut (4:00 pm)
Meet with Billy's teacher (4:30 pm)
Lunch with Joan (12:00 noon at the City Cafe)

Questions

1. When is dinner with the Wilsons?

2. When is the picnic at the lake?

3. Are there any things that are scheduled at the same time?

4. Do you have anything scheduled on the 18th? 26th? 7th?

5. Which Friday are you going to the theater?

6. When is your haircut?

7. When and what time is your doctor appointment?

8. What are the dates of the First Aid course?

9. Do you have an appointment with the dentist?

Form B

Directions: Work with a partner. Each partner has a calendar and a list of events. You are partner B. Write the following six events somewhere on your calendar. Tell your partner where to write these events on her calendar. Don't look at each other's calendars! Partner A will tell you six more events to add to your calendar. Please listen and write them in. When you are finished, look at your calendars together and answer the questions. Write your answers.

Calendar Events for Partner B

John's surprise birthday party (Saturday at 6:00 pm)
Picnic at the lake
First Aid course (every Wednesday at 6:00 pm)
Theater (Friday night at 8:00 pm)
Dinner at Bill's
Doctor appointment (Tuesday at 3:00 pm)

Questions

1. When is dinner with the Wilsons?

2. When is the picnic at the lake?

3. Are there any things that are scheduled at the same time?

4. Do you have anything scheduled on the 18th? 26th? 7th?

5. Which Friday are you going to the theater?

6. When is your haircut?

7. When and what time is your doctor appointment?

8. What are the dates of the First Aid course?

9. Do you have an appointment with the dentist?

SUN	MON	TUE	WED	THU	FRI	SAT
				1	2	3
4	5	6	7	8	9	10
11	12	13	14	15	16	17
18	19	20	21	22	23	24
25	26	27	28	29	30	31

Students work in pairs. Each student has a calendar page. Partner A has Dictation Sheet A, Partner B has Dictation Sheet B. Partner A dictates six dates to his partner, saying: "Make an X on Monday, July 8." or "Make a circle around Wednesday, August 14." Partner B then dictates her dates, Partner A follows the instructions. When complete, do a self-check.

Sample 9
CHARTS
AND GRIDS

Calendar
Dictation

Dictation Sheet A
Tell your partner to put an "X" on:
    Monday, July 8
    Wednesday, August 14
    Saturday, September 28
Tell your partner to circle:
    Sunday, October 10
    Tuesday, November 5
    Thursday, December 12

Dictation Sheet B
Tell your partner to put an "X" on:
    Monday, July 29
    Wednesday, August 7
    Friday, September 20
Tell your partner to circle:
    Thursday, October 31
    Saturday, November 2
    Tuesday, December 23

---

1. January

S	M	T	W	T	F	S
		1	2	3	4	5
6	7	8	9	10	11	12
13	14	15	16	17	18	19
20	21	22	23	24	25	26
27	28	29	30	31		

2. February

S	M	T	W	T	F	S
					1	2
3	4	5	6	7	8	9
10	11	12	13	14	15	16
17	18	19	20	21	22	23
24	25	26	27	28		

3. March

S	M	T	W	T	F	S
					1	2
3	4	5	6	7	8	9
10	11	12	13	14	15	16
17	18	19	20	21	22	23
24/31	25	26	27	28	29	30

4. April

S	M	T	W	T	F	S
	1	2	3	4	5	6
7	8	9	10	11	12	13
14	15	16	17	18	19	20
21	22	23	24	25	26	27
28	29	30				

5. May

S	M	T	W	T	F	S
			1	2	3	4
5	6	7	8	9	10	11
12	13	14	15	16	17	18
19	20	21	22	23	24	25
26	27	28	29	30	31	

6. June

S	M	T	W	T	F	S
						1
2	3	4	5	6	7	8
9	10	11	12	13	14	15
16	17	18	19	20	21	22
23/30	24	25	26	27	28	29

7. July

S	M	T	W	T	F	S
	1	2	3	4	5	6
7	8	9	10	11	12	13
14	15	16	17	18	19	20
21	22	23	24	25	26	27
28	29	30	31			

8. August

S	M	T	W	T	F	S
				1	2	3
4	5	6	7	8	9	10
11	12	13	14	15	16	17
18	19	20	21	22	23	24
25	26	27	28	29	30	31

9. September

S	M	T	W	T	F	S
1	2	3	4	5	6	7
8	9	10	11	12	13	14
15	16	17	18	19	20	21
22	23	24	25	26	27	28
29	30					

10. October

S	M	T	W	T	F	S
		1	2	3	4	5
6	7	8	9	10	11	12
13	14	15	16	17	18	19
20	21	22	23	24	25	26
27	28	29	30	31		

11. November

S	M	T	W	T	F	S
					1	2
3	4	5	6	7	8	9
10	11	12	13	14	15	16
17	18	19	20	21	22	23
24	25	26	27	28	29	30

12. December

S	M	T	W	T	F	S
1	2	3	4	5	6	7
8	9	10	11	12	13	14
15	16	17	18	19	20	21
22	23	24	25	26	27	28
29	30	31				

**Sample 10
CHARTS
AND GRIDS**

Personal Grid

Directions: Each student receives a blank grid. The teacher dictates questions and the students write the questions anywhere they want in the grid. All the questions are about the students themselves.

Questions for dictation.

1. What is your favorite TV show?
2. What are your hobbies?
3. Who is one person you admire?
4. What is your favorite place to visit?
5. What kind of work would you most like to do?
6. What kind of food would you most like to have for dinner?
7. Who is one person you trust?
8. What is one thing you would like to buy?
9. What are five things you have that you really like?

After all the questions have been written on the grids, students take turns interviewing a partner. They write short notes in the grid. Each student should ask all questions. They can then use the grid to write a paragraph about what they learned.

1.	2.	3.
4.	5.	6.
7.	8.	9.

MISSING PARTS, DIFFERENT PIECES

General procedures

Students work together in three ways to supply missing information. They use dialogs, readings, and group dictation. With dialogs, students are given visual cues that are complete and asked to supply dialogs based on what they think the characters in the pictures are saying. In readings, they are given the text that is complete and asked to work together to solve the problem. The answer is the missing part. With group dictation, the teacher prepares two or three different versions of the same text for a cloze activity. Each text is incomplete. The two or three different versions together provide the complete text. The teacher deliberately dictates the information too fast for the students to record. Students are not able to get all of the information. When the students join together, they have the necessary information to complete all of the cloze spaces.

The instructor prepares beforehand two drawings that are the same except for five to ten minor differences. (These drawings may be taken from magazines or cartoons and then altered slightly with liquid paper correction fluid and black pen.) Students work in pairs. Student A gets picture A and Student B gets picture B. They are not to look at each others' pictures. A file folder standing on end between them hides their view. Students are instructed to describe the pictures to each other and come up with 10 differences between them. This should be a time limit activity because some students will work much faster than others.

**Sample 1
MISSING PARTS, DIFFERENT PIECES**

What's the Difference?

A

B

Sample 2
MISSING PARTS, DIFFERENT PIECES

Tell It Like It Is

For this activity, the instructor prepares only one drawing and duplicates it. This drawing is given to Student A who will describe it very carefully to Student B so that Student B can draw an exact copy. A file folder should be standing on end between the partners. They should be instructed not to look! After a set time period, have the students remove the barriers to see how close the drawings are. Have them describe the differences to you.

Sample 3
MISSING PARTS, DIFFERENT PIECES

Problem Solving

Give each student a copy of the text and the diagram below. Ask the students to work individually at first. They should read the text, determine which dinner guest is seated in which chair, and write their names around the table. After they have worked about 15 minutes, have them pair up with another person and compare answers. Once they agree on their answers, have them join another pair and compare answers. Together in their small groups, they should practice explaining why they made the choices they did based on the text.

Dinner with the Andersons

In the center of the table was a small glass vase with four red carnations, tidily arranged. Nancy Anderson was a women who loved to have everything in order. The carnations were arranged like four points on the compass - the north, south, east, and west. Around this carnation-pointed compass, the guests were to be seated. Deciding on how to arrange the guests had not been easy for Nancy Anderson, but Nancy had arrived at the perfect solution. She put the "talkers" opposite each other, and the "non-talkers" between them. In this way, she was sure at least that the conversation would be directed towards the center, and not away from it. Nancy had systematically divided the guests into those who talked "too much" and those who talked "too little."

The night of the dinner party arrived. Nancy looked down the long table and saw with pleasure that her planning had worked. She was right. The "talkers" were talking, the "non-talkers" were listening. She felt great pride in having distributed the people so well. At each corner of the table was a talker; between each talker were two non-talkers; and, at either end, like two magnetic poles, the host and hostess, Nancy and Bill Anderson.

Two conversations were going at once. She sat back and listened. "It's not the first time; things have disappeared before..." Jerry Fowlings, who with every word moved his knife closer to Nancy's fork, was explaining his theory to the Dicksons while from the opposite corner, Antony Vandergard (whom Nancy called "my left hand man") was explaining his theory to the Madisons. "A professional thief would never have used dynamite..." Silent and respectful, the two married couples stared at each other over the carnations. But before they could say anything, two other voices had broken into the conversation. Peter Mikes like a warm wind from the southwest, said cheerfully, "Well, they didn't take everything, did they?" And Jean Guys, like a cold blast from the northwest, answered, "What makes you so sure that they did it?"

Nancy Anderson was pleased and happy. This was what she had wanted.

Dinner with the Anderson's Diagram

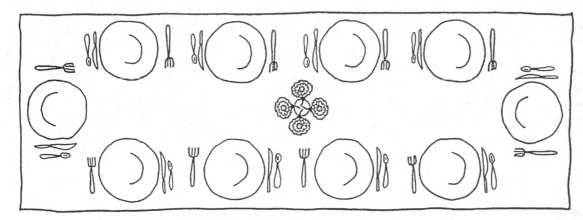

The teacher should make copies of Cloze #1 and Cloze #2 for half of the class. Have the students work with a partner. Each person will receive one handout prepared for cloze activity. The teacher gives the dictation. Students will not be able to get all of the information. Rather than repeat the dictation, ask the students to join with another member of the class. Each pair should have a #1 and a #2. Students work with each other to find the information they are missing. Together, they have the completed text. When the groups believe they have all of the information, the teacher should read the material again.

**Sample 4
MISSING
PARTS,
DIFFERENT
PIECES**

Group Dictation

Cloze Activity #1 Form A

At seventeen years old, Bill Nichols knew exactly what he wanted to do. He wanted to sail
_____. He had been sailing small boats since _____, and at seventeen he
felt ready to sail alone around the world.

Bill set sail _____, _____, on a ship he named Dove. His uncle gave him two
kittens to keep him company. The seventeen-year-old was _____ the kittens because
after one day at _____ he was ready to turn around and _____. Only a sudden
storm made Bill forget his loneliness and gave him the ambition to _____.

_____ was Bill's first stop. It took him 22 days to reach _____ from
California. This was only the beginning of a trip around the world. _____, Bill
was back out _____ continuing his journey.

There were other lonely nights, _____, sharks, running low on food, and
_____ to deal with. Through a combination of skill and luck Bill was able to
handle all the problems. When he stopped at _____, like Pago Pago, the Friendly
Islands, and Fiji, he was _____. They invited him to share their food
and stories. Bill learned a great deal about _____ and _____ from these new
friends. He stayed in some places _____. On one of the islands
Bill met _____ named Patti. They became friends, and spent a lot of time
_____. When it was time for Bill to leave the islands, he and Patti _____ spots on
his sailing route where they could meet. They met first in _____. There they
_____; Bill was now _____. They spent their honeymoon _____,
camping and sightseeing in Africa's lion and rhinoceros country.

Cloze Activity #2 Form B

At seventeen years old, Bill Nichols knew _____. He wanted to _____ around the world. He had been sailing small boats since he was ten, and _____ to sail alone around the world.

Bill set sail on July 27, 1985, _____.

His uncle gave him two kittens _____. The seventeen-year-old was glad to have the kittens because after only one day at sea he was ready to turn around and come home._____ _____and gave him ambition to continue on this trip.

Hawaii was Bill's _____. It took him 22 days to reach Hawaii from California. _____ _____. After a few days in Hawaii, Bill was back out in the Pacific _____
_____.

There were other lonely nights, storms, sharks, _____, and other sea enemies to deal with. _____ Bill was able to handle all the problems.
_____
_____ at islands in the Pacific Ocean, like Pago Pago and Fiji, _____ by the island people. _____ to share their food and stories. Bill learned a great deal about different _____ their cultures from these new friends. _____ even months.

_____ Bill met an American girl named Patti. They became friends, _____ together. When it was time for Bill to leave _____, he and Patti picked out spots on his sailing _____ could meet. They met _____. There, they got married; Bill was now 18 years old. _____ on a motorcycle, camping and sightseeing in Africa's _____ country.

Group Dictation Script

At seventeen years old, Bill Nichols knew exactly what he wanted to do. He wanted to sail around the world. He had been sailing small boats since he was ten, and at seventeen he felt ready to sail alone around the world.

Bill set sail July 27, 1985, on a ship he named Dove. His uncle gave him two kittens to keep him company. The seventeen-year-old was glad to have the kittens because after one day at sea he was ready to turn around and come home. Only a sudden storm made Bill forget his loneliness and gave him the ambition to continue on his trip.

Hawaii was Bill's first stop. It took him 22 days to reach Hawaii from California. This was only the beginning of a trip around the world. After a few days in Hawaii, Bill was back out in the Pacific, continuing his journey around the world.

There were other lonely nights, storms, sharks, running low on food, and other sea enemies to deal with. Through a combination of skill and luck Bill was able to handle all the problems. When he stopped at islands in the Pacific Ocean, like Pago Pago, the Friendly Islands, and Fiji, he was welcomed by the island people. They invited him to share their food and stories. Bill learned a great deal about different people and their cultures from these new friends. He stayed in some places for weeks and even months.

On one of the islands Bill met an American girl named Patti. They became friends, and spent a lot of time together. When it was time for Bill to leave the islands, he and Patti picked out spots on his sailing route where they could meet. They met first in Australia. There they got married; Bill was now 18 years old. They spent their honeymoon on a motorcycle, camping and sightseeing in Africa's lion and rhinoceros country.

**Sample 5
MISSING
PARTS,
DIFFERENT
PIECES**

Cartoon Dialog

Directions: Work with a partner, write what you think the people in this dialog are saying. Then practice the dialog together and be prepared to present it to the class.

1.

2.

Student A reads what is on her card. Student B writes it on his paper. They compare. Then, Student B reads his card and Student A writes it on her paper.

Example Dictation Pairs　　　　　*Beginning*

**Sample 6
MISSING
PARTS,
DIFFERENT
PIECES**

Dictation Pairs

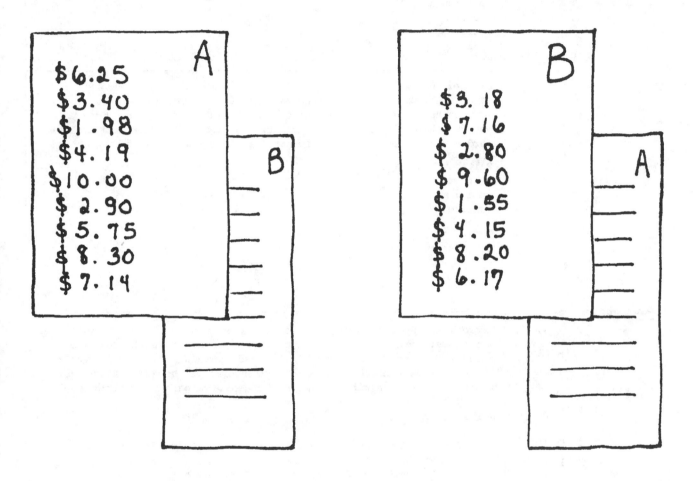

Try the following content for beginning students:
　　　numbers
　　　prices
　　　phone numbers
　　　time
　　　spelling out words "c-l-o-c-k" or "d-o-o-r"
　　　dictating simple words
　　　dates

Example Dictation Pairs   *Advanced*

```
Partner A
Directions: Dictate the four words below to your partner. Don't show
your partner the words. Your partner will dictate four words to you.
When you have finished, pronounce the eight words together and use the
words in a sentence. If you are not sure of the meaning, make a guess!

Partner A Dictates
commitment
receive
beard
ceiling
```

```
Partner B
Directions: Dictate the four words below to your partner. Don't show
your partner the words. Your partner will dictate four words to you.
When you have finished, pronounce the eight words together and use the
words in a sentence. If you are not sure of the meaning, make a guess!

Partner B Dictates
believe
embarrass
lonesome
suitcase
```

Sample 7 MISSING PARTS, DIFFERENT PIECES

Sentence Dictation

```
Directions: Work in groups of four. Choose a group leader. The leader
has the sentence list, Worksheet A.  The others have the picture
page, Worksheet B.  Partner A will read sentence #1.  The others will
listen to the sentences and mark the number "1" beside the correct
picture.  Continue with all 16 sentences.  Compare your answers.

Worksheet A

 1.  The teacher rang the bell loudly, but the children paid no
     attention.
 2.  I had a small gold whistle when I was a child.
 3.  I watch the news on television every morning.
 4.  The door squeaks when it opens and closes.
 5.  If I want to get up early in the morning, I will have to use my
     alarm clock to wake me.
 6.  The water is dripping from the faucet in the kitchen.
 7.  If I had a hammer and a small nail, I could hang the picture for
     you.
 8.  She had been typing on that manuscript for about eight hours.
 9.  He had been expecting a call from his wife all afternoon.
10.  We found an old phonograph player in the attic.
11.  Did you find your keys finally?
12.  There is a pencil sharpener in the office on the second floor.
13.  Please staple the exam sheets together by 1:30 pm today.
14.  We clapped loudly for the musician.
15.  This call is for you. Can you take it?
16.  You will need some wood and a saw to finish the project.
```

Worksheet B

Directions: Work in groups of four. Choose a group leader. The leader has the sentence list, Worksheet A. The others have the picture page, Worksheet B. The leader will read sentence #1. The others will listen to the sentences and mark the number "1" beside the correct picture. Continue with all 16 sentences. Compare your answers.

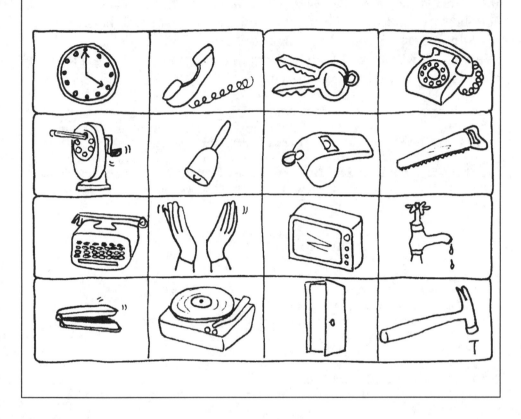

PAPER SEARCH

General procedures

In these activities, the focus is on scanning pictures and using the information in a variety of ways. Students are encouraged to use the information they get to guess and arrive at an answer. In a collaborative classroom, students can take the responsibility for bringing newspapers and magazines to class. You may also supplement what the students bring, but they should not be left out of the task of finding picture sources.

**Sample 1
PAPER SEARCH**

Newspaper Scan

Directions: You and your classmates should bring about a week of newspapers to class. Work in small groups. Each group should have one copy of the handout. Search for the following things in the newspaper. When you find an item, cut it out, number it, and cross the item off of your list.

Group List for Newspaper Search
 1. An ad for an unfurnished apartment
 2. An ad for a used car
 3. An article about football
 4. An article about the president of the United States
 5. An article about a world leader
 6. An article about travel
 7. An ad for a movie
 8. An ad for a concert
 9. An ad for groceries
10. Some news about the weather
11. Some news about something that will happen in the future
12. Some news about a foreign country
13. Some good news
14. Some bad news

Magazine Scan

Directions: You and your classmates bring several magazines to class. Work together in small groups of three or four. Find pictures of 15 different items, cut them out, and paste them on white paper.

Then, trade pictures with another group. Do not look at your new pictures. Keep them face down.

Then, one person at a time chooses a picture from the pile. That person will not show the picture to the rest of the people in the group. The task of the group will be to ask questions in order to guess what is on the card. It is OK to give hints or clues after 10 questions have been asked.

Bring old magazines to class. Ask each person to find a picture of an interesting person, cut it out, and mount it on plain, white paper. Divide students into groups of six. Begin by asking students the first question on the list below. Tell them there are no wrong answers. They may write anything they think is true or a good answer. Ask them to write the answer on the back of their pictures. Then have them pass their pictures one to the left. They look at their new picture and read what has been written. Then ask the second question. They write an answer for the new question. After they have answered the second question, they pass the pictures one to the left again. After all questions have been answered, they pass the picture to the left one more time. When all group members have their original pictures back, they take turns reading the stories aloud in their groups.

```
Questions for Who Am I?
   a. What is this person's name? How old is s/he?
      Where does s/he live?
   b. What kind of work does this person do?
   c. What is this person's family like?
   d. What are this person's hobbies?
   e. Name one thing this person likes. Name one thing
      this person hates.
Now work with your original picture and story. Correct
errors, revise and polish it. Copy it over in your best
handwriting. Post it in the classroom next to the
picture!
```

Students will work in small groups of 3 - 5 students. Each group chooses one person to be the secretary. Only that person should write. Give each group pictures of several houses to describe. As a group, the students should decide on answers to the questions below. When individual groups have finished answering questions about the first house, they can continue with another house. Let the groups know when their time is up.

```
Questions for Who Lives Here?

1. As a group write a description of the house.
2. Where is the house?
3. What is good about living in this house?
4. What is not so good about living in this house?
5. Would you like to live here? Why or Why not?

Find another group who described your same house.
Did you have similar answers? Different answers?
```

Sample 5
PAPER SEARCH
Search and Find

Give students a magazine or newspaper ad (or let them choose their own). In pairs or individually, students will look for words they know and circle them. They can read the words out loud and then copy them onto a piece of paper.

Panasonic introduces the new Palmcorder Camcorder with Digital Image Stabilization.

Watching a video tape shouldn't be a game of follow the bouncing baby. All too often it is, because most people have trouble holding a camcorder steady. And when your hand shakes so does the picture. That's why the new PV-53 Panasonic Palmcorder Camcorder has DEIS—Digital Electronic Image Stabilization. It helps hold the picture steady.

And DEIS is just the beginning of this camcorder's advanced technology. It has a color viewfinder. A 20X digital zoom. And special effects like digital wipes and fades. Plus it's controlled by a remote that's smaller than a credit card. But most importantly, the Panasonic Palmcorder Camcorder lets you watch tapes in any VHS recorder with its included PlayPak. Yours, your family's or any of the 70 million out there. That makes showing your tapes and sharing them incredibly easy. The new Panasonic Palmcorder. It helps hold the picture steady when you can't. Its tapes play in your VCR. The choice is obvious. ❑

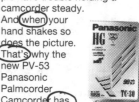

Panasonic compact VHS tapes record for up to 1½ hours.

How many words do you know? Make a circle. Read aloud. Copy eight.

The PlayPak lets you play your tapes in any VHS recorder. Yours, your family's and your friends.'

THIS NEW PANASONIC PALMCORDER™ HELPS HOLD THE PICTURE STEADY EVEN WHEN YOUR HAND SHAKES.

Advertisement Courtesy of Matsushita Consumer Electronics Company

Panasonic
just slightly ahead of our time®

WORD GAMES

General procedures

The stimulus for these activities is a word. You can use words that students have been working with in class or choose a word that might be new to them.

Students work in pairs. Prepare 1 copy of the grid for each pair of students. Set a time limit for this activity of ten minutes. Give each pair the same word to begin with. Longer, polysyllabic words work best such as encyclopedia, dictionary, association, acquisition, prediction, transportation, etc. One partner writes this word down the middle of the grid, one letter per square (see example).

Rules:
1) Partners take turns adding any words they choose, crossword fashion.
2) All words must connect.
3) All contiguous letters must form words.

When the time limit is up, have the group with the most words share their answers. Find out how the crosswords are different.

Sample 1
WORD GAMES

Crossword Making

Sample 2
WORD GAMES

Crossword Themes

This activity works best if students have all done crossword puzzles before. Give them a sample to do first before you have them try making their own. Give students a theme or topic they are familiar with and have been studying in class. Have them make a crossword puzzle with words related to that theme. Give each group a sheet of the grid. Have them share their puzzles with another group when they have finished.

Steps:

a. Determine how the words can connect.

b. Make a sample puzzle with the words only.

Additional Steps for More Advanced Students:

c. Give the words numbers.

d. Decide how many clues you need for down and across and make the corresponding numbers.

e. Write the clues.

Possible themes include going to the doctor, reading the want ads, vacations, sports and fun, home and family, places in the community.

Have students work in pairs or small groups. This is a timed activity. They should work with each word for five minutes. Give each group the same word, e.g. dictionary. Have them try to form as many different words as they can using the letters in the word given. After five minutes, have them stop and give them a new word. When the time is finished, have them count how many words they have made. Ask the group with the most words to put their list on the board.

Sample 3
WORD GAMES

Words Within Words

Have students work in pairs or small groups. They should choose a secretary. The secretary will get the crossword puzzle. The other members of the group will get the questions. Only the secretary can write on the puzzle. The other group members must tell the secretary what to write and where to put the answer.

Sample 4
WORD GAMES

Crossword Puzzles

Mindscape Educational Software makes a piece of excellent (and fun!) software entitled *Crossword Magic* for crossword puzzle making. See the citation in the bibliography for complete information

Example Crossword Puzzle   The United States

Across Clues

3. A Southern state that does not border the Gulf of Mexico
5. The largest continental state
9. Borders on a large lake
12. A southern state bordered by South Carolina and the Atlantic Ocean (2 words)
13. Islands in the Pacific Ocean
14. A southern state east of Texas
16. Divided by a large lake
17. West of Utah and east of California

Down Clues

1. West of Nevada, bordering the Pacific Ocean
2. The most northeastern state
4. Surrounded on three sides by water
6. The largest state
7. Between Nevada and Colorado
8. Next to the Canadian border
10. Settled by the Pilgrims in 1620
11. In the most northwest corner
15. Includes New York City (2 words)

☞ *For your convenience, answers for the crossword puzzles on pages 116, 119, 118, and 119 can be found on page 124.*

Example Crossword Puzzle   *Clothes*

Across Clues

2. We wear these on our feet when the weather is warm.
4. You need this when the weather is very cold.
5. A t-shirt is often worn with _____.
7. He wears these shoes for walking.
9. In the fall and winter, many people wear _____.
11. These are worn on the feet.
12. There's a button missing from my _____.
14. A _____ is worn around the waist.

Down Clues

1. This is often worn with a skirt.
2. This is worn under a skirt.
3. It is chilly. You may need a _____.
6. She bought a new _____ to wear to the concert.
7. This goes around the neck.
8. These are usually worn over socks.
9. This is often worn with a blouse.
10. He must wear a _____ to work everyday.
13. A _____ is often worn with Levis.

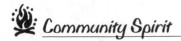

Example Crossword Puzzle   Things at School

Across Clues

2. Don't use a pen, use a _____.
4. I am reading a good _____.
5. I am almost out of _____. I need to go to the bookstore to buy more.
6. Used to hang pictures.
8. I write notes in this.
9. The teacher is writing on the _____.
11. Many books are in this building.
14. May I use the _____ to call my family?
15. He _____ the pages of the lesson together so that we wouldn't lose them.
16. She has a new box of _____. There are 48 colors in her box.
17. There are eight students and one _____ in the classroom.
18. There are 20 _____ and 22 students in the classroom.
19. How many _____ are there in your school?

Down Clues

1. The student is seated at a _____.
3. I need a _____ to help me with my homework.
7. You use this to clean the blackboard.
10. The teacher give us _____ every night.
12. I buy books here.
13. There are eight _____ and one teacher in the classroom.

Example Crossword Puzzle The U.S. Government

Across Clues

3. The legislative branch is sometimes called _____.
6. The President is the head of this branch.
9. This branch makes the law.
10. This house in Congress has equal representation from each state.
11. The executive branch enforces the _____.
12. The president is elected to a 4-year _____.
13. Changes to the Constitution are called _____.
15. There are two _____ in Congress.
16. There are three _____ in the United States Government.

Down Clues

1. This branch judges the laws.
2. A _____ can become law.
4. This member of Congress is elected to a 2-year term.
5. The highest court is the _____ _____. (2 words)
7. Senators are _____ to 6-year terms.
8. This person is head of the executive branch.
14. There are nine of these on the Supremo Court.

**Sample 5
WORD GAMES**

**What Do
You See?**

Hand out the picture to pairs of students. Partner A says the name of an item in the picture. Partner B writes down what A has said.

What do you see?

1. _____	5. _____	9. _____
2. _____	6. _____	10. _____
3. _____	7. _____	11. _____
4. _____	8. _____	12. _____

Bibliography

Bassano, S. and M.A. Christison, 1992. *Drawing Out.* Englewood Cliffs, New Jersey USA: Prentice Hall Regents.

Bassano, S., 1993. *First Class Reader.* San Francisco, California USA: Alta Book Center, Publishers.

Bassano, S., 1980. *Sounds Easy.* Englewood Cliffs, New Jersey USA: Alemany Press, Prentice Hall Regents.

Beckerman, H. S., 1991. *Heartworks: Inspirations for English as a Second Language.* Englewood Cliffs, New Jersey USA: Prentice Hall Regents.

Bejarano, Y., 1987. A cooperative, small-group methodology in the language classroom. *TESOL Quarterly,* 21(3), 483-504.

Beyer, M., et al 1981. *Verbs, Verbs, Verbs.* Austin, Texas USA: Pro-Ed Company.

Byrd, D. R. H. and John Klosek, 1991. *Can We Talk?* Englewood Cliffs, New Jersey USA: Prentice Hall Regents.

Byrd, D. R. H. and I. Clemente-Cabetas, 1980. *React-Interact.* Englewood Cliffs, New Jersey USA: Prentice Hall Regents.

Christison, M. A. and S. Bassano, 1987. *Look Who's Talking.* Englewood Cliffs, New Jersey USA: Alemany Press, Prentice Hall Regents.

Christison, M.A. and S. Bassano, 1987. *Purple Cows and Potato Chips.* Englewood Cliffs, New Jersey USA: Alemany Press, Prentice Hall Regents.

Cohen, E., 1986. *Designing Group Work: Strategies for the Heterogeneous Classroom.* New York USA: Columbia University, Teachers College Press.

Crossword Magic, 1985 (with version updates). Chicago, Illinois USA: Mindscape Educational Software, SVE (Society for Visual Education).

DeAvila, E., S. Duncan, and C.J. Navarette, 1987. *Finding out /Descubrimiento: Teacher's Resource Guide.* Northvale, New Jersey USA: Santillana.

Freiere, P., 1981. *Pedagogy of the Oppressed.* New York, USA: Continuum Publishing Corporation.

Gaies, S., 1985. *Peer Involvement in Language Learning.* Englewood Cliffs, New Jersey USA: Prentice Hall Regents/Center for Applied Linguistics.

Harklau, Linda., 1994. ESL versus mainstream classes: Contrasting L2 learning environments. 1994. *TESOL Quarterly,* Vol 28. No. 2 pp.241-272.

Illich, I., 1971. *Deschooling Society.* New York, USA: Harper and Row.

Johnson, D.W. and F.P. Johnson, 1987. *Joining Together: Group Theory and Group Skills.* Englewood Cliffs, New Jersey USA: Prentice Hall Regents/Center for Applied Linguistics.

Kagan, S., 1989. *Cooperative Learning.* Capistrano, California USA: Resources for Teachers.

Kagan, S., 1986. Cooperative learning and sociocultural factors in schooling. In California State Department of Education, *Beyond Language: Social and Cultural Factors in Schooling Language Minority Students* (pp. 231-198). Los Angeles, California USA: Evaluation, Dissemination and Assessment Center, California State University.

Klippel, F., 1985. *Keep Talking: Communicative Fluency Activities for Language Teaching.* New York, USA: Cambridge University Press.

Krashen, S. and T. Terrell, 1983. *The Natural Approach: Language Acquisition in the Classroom.* Englewood Cliffs, New Jersey USA: Prentice Hall Regents.

Larsen-Freeman, Diane and Michael H. Long, 1991. *An Introduction to Second Language Research.* New York, NY: Longman, Inc. pp. 220-296.

Leibowitz, D., 1980. *Basic Vocabulary Builder,* Lincolnwood, Illinois USA: National Textbook Co.

Little, L.W. and I.A. Greenberg, 1991. *Problem Solving: Critical Thinking and Communication Skills.* New York, USA: Longman Publishers.

Long, M. and P. Porter, 1985. Group work, interlanguage talk, and second laguage acquisition. *TESOL Quarterly,* 19(2), 207-228.

Long, M., 1981. Input, interaction, and second-language acquisition. *Annals of the New York Academy of Sciences,* 379, 207-278.

Long, M., 1980. Groupwork and communicative competence in the ESOL classroom. *TESOL Newsletter,* June. Vol. 14.

McGroarty, M. 1991. Cooperative learning: The benefits for content-area teaching. In P.A Richard-Amato and M.A. Snow (Eds.), *The Multicultural Classroom.* White Plains, USA: Longman Publishers.

Nunan, David, 1989. *Understanding Language Classrooms: A Guide for Teacher-Initiated Action.* Hertfordshire, UK: Regents/Prentice Hall. New Jersey USA pp. 36-54.

Olsen, J.W.-B., 1984. *Look Again Pictures for Language Development and Lifeskills.* Englewood Cliffs, New Jersey USA: Prentice Hall Regents.

Pack, A. T. and D. Dillon, 1980. Peer tutoring activities for the ESL classroom. *TESOL Newsletter,* June. Vol. 15.

Palmer, A. and T. Rodgers, and J.W.-B. Olsen, 1985. *Back and Forth.* Englewood Cliffs, New Jersey USA: Prentice Hall Regents, Alemany Press.

Pica, Teresa 1994. Questions from the language classroom: Research perspectives. *TESOL Quarterly.* Volume 28, Number 1. pp. 49-79.

Rooks, G.M., 1988. *Non-stop Discussion Workbook.* Boston, Massachusetts USA: Heinle & Heinle.

Rooks, G.M., 1983. *Can't Stop Talking.* Boston, Massachusetts USA: Heinle & Heinle.

Sadow, S., 1982. *Idea Bank.* Boston, Massachusetts USA: Heinle & Heinle.

Simon, S., L. Howe, and H. Kirschebaum, 1978., *Values Clarification: A Handbook of Practical Strategies,* New York, USA: Hart Publishers.

Sion, C., ed., 1985. *Recipes for Tired Teachers.* Redwood City, California USA: Addison Wesley Publishers.

Stevick, E., 1980. *Teaching Languages: A Way and Ways.* Boston, Massachusetts USA: Heinle & Heinle.

Swain, M., 1985. Communicative competence: Some roles of comprehensible input and comprehensive output in its development. In S. Gass and C. Madden (Eds.), *Input in Second Language Acquisition,* 235-253. Boston, Massachusetts USA: Heinle & Heinle.

Ur, Penny, 1981. *Discussions That Work: Task-centered Fluency Practice.* New York, USA: Cambridge University Press.

Williams, Constance, 1989. *Write on to Reading: A Resource Book of Critical and Creative Writing Activities.* Menlo Park, CA: Williams-Williams Publishers.

Witbeck, M., 1976. Peer correction procedures for intermediate and advanced ESL composition lessons. *TESOL Quarterly,* September, 10(3), 321-326.

Yorkey, R., 1985. *Talk-a-tivities.* Redwood City, California USA: Addison Wesley Publishers.

Zelman, N. E., 1986. *Conversation Inspirations.* Brattelboro, Vermont USA: Pro Lingua Associates.

Answers to Crossword Puzzles

Page 116, *The United States*

Across	Down
3. Arkansas	1. California
5. Texas	2. Maine
9. Ohio	4. Florida
12. North Carolina	6. Alaska
13. Hawaii	7. Utah
14. Louisiana	8. Montana
16. Michigan	10. Massachusetts
17. Nevada	11. Washington
	15. New York

Page 118, *Things at School*

Across	Down
2. pencil	1. desk
4. book	2. computer
5. paper	7. eraser
6. tape	10. homework
8. notebook	12. bookstore
9. blackboard	13. students
11. library	
14. telephone	
15. stapled	
16. crayons	
17. teacher	
18. chairs	
19. classrooms	

Page 117, *Clothes*

Across	Down
2. sandals	1. blouse
4. coat	2. slip
5. Levis	3. jacket
7. tennis shoes	6. dress
9. sweaters	7. tie
11. shoes	8. shoes
12. shirt	9. skirt
14. belt	10. suit
	13. t-shirt

Page 119, *The U.S. Government*

Across	Down
3. Congress	1. Judicial
6. Executive	2. bill
9. Legislative	4. Representative
10. Senate	5. Supreme Court
11. laws	7. elected
12. term	8. President
13. amendments	14. judges
15. houses	
16. branches	